Junípero Serra

A Pictorial Biography

By

Martin J. Morgado

Siempre Adelante Publishing
1190 Alta Mesa Road
Monterey, California 93940

Library of Congress Catalog Card Number: 90-62288
ISBN 0-9627216-0-3

First edition, first printing.

Front cover: The Querétaro Serra Portrait (see illustration 119).
Back cover: Pope John Paul II at Junípero Serra's grave (see illustration 140).

Preface

When first drawn to Junípero Serra's California home, mission headquarters and burial place at Mission San Carlos Borromeo del Río Carmelo, I was fascinated with artifacts linked directly to Serra, the state's founder and candidate for Catholic sainthood. However, most were simply labeled "used by" or "owned by Father Serra." Turning to the plethora of Serran literature, I found many books about the man, but none about what the man left behind. Therefore, the main purpose of this book is to identify and document Serra's possessions and physical environment that are still in existence today, within an accurate Serra biography and well-illustrated format. Since his Franciscan vows bound him to "living without property," he literally owned nothing and "possessions" refer only to what he touched, used and valued as the tools of his missionary ministry.

The major problem with such an inquiry is verification. As a result of early-nineteenth-century secularization of church property in Majorca, Mexico and California, many artifacts familiar to Serra were dispersed, altered or destroyed. In Mexico today, little remains except church structures. Majorca fared better, and has reclaimed much of its patrimony.

In California, 1884 marked the centennial of Serra's death, and publication of Helen Hunt Jackson's widely-read romantic novel *Ramona*. In the surge of nostalgia that followed, California's founding and early development were idealized as a "Spanish Arcadia" with Serra at the helm and personally responsible for every detail. We still bear this distorted legacy, for in missions and museums the length of the state, one finds crosses/crucifixes, statues, vestments, chalices, books, chairs, even a bookmark and locket casually claimed to have been brought here and used by Serra.

With chain of provenance broken and innumerable legends filling the void, documentation is the only way of disentangling fact from fiction. For example, Serra received a monstrance for Mission Carmel in 1778, a gift from New Spain's Viceroy Bucareli. The correspondence, receipt, and even Serra's thank-you note for "so precious a prize" still exist in Mexico City's Archivo de la Nación. In addition, the monstrance is inscribed and hallmarked.

Documentation can also disprove. Simply because a Mission Carmel chalice is strikingly similar in design to the Bucareli Monstrance, both were historically assumed to be gifts of Bucareli and thereby present in Serra's day. Unfortunately, documentation and hallmark research proved the chalice did not arrive at Mission Carmel until twenty years after his death. An ensuing search for a true "Serra chalice" at another mission, museum or in a private collection proved futile, and at this point it cannot be stated that California possesses a chalice used by Serra.

When documentation does not exist, alternate methods of verification must be used. For example, Mission Carmel's "Serra Indian Reliquary" was thought to have been made by an Indian craftsman for Serra. There is no written proof. However, among local Spanish and Indian families there was a great weight of tradition that it was used by Serra, and the contents also point toward such: a wax *Agnus Dei* from the pontificate of Pius VI, a contemporary of Serra; a relic of Saint Francis Solano, Serra's favorite saint; and most importantly, the handwritten descriptions on both sides. After consulting with a court-certified documents and handwriting expert, the conclusion was drawn that Serra had written the descriptions.

If documentation or alternate methods are unavailable, it is virtually impossible to definitively link an artifact to Serra. For example, after the Mission Carmel chalice mentioned above was discounted as Serra's, an alternate Mission Carmel candidate was brought forward, claimed to have been Serra's and consequently used by His Holiness Pope John Paul II when he celebrated Mass in Monterey on 17 September 1987. With the help of a professional appraiser/antiquarian specializing in silver, the undocumented, unmarked chalice was found to be late-eighteenth-century Mexican silver. Beyond that, Serra *may* have used it.

The scope of this book includes every item found to date and proved to have been personally used by Serra. Also, anything he ordered for a California mission or that was present in his day and survives. All extant physical structures that figured prominently in his life are also featured. Photographs of the present façades of Serra's nine California missions are included as reference point, because the original buildings have all been replaced (at least the consecrated sites are the same, with the exception of Mission Santa Clara, moved to another site after his death). Only Mission San Juan Capistrano's "Serra Chapel" partially dates from his period, and is featured in greater detail.

The buildings and artifacts, presented chronologically as they entered Serra's life, are also discussed apart from him as independent works of art. Their present location is listed in parentheses at the end of the corresponding caption. Unusual foreign words are translated and technical terms defined the first time they appear in the text, and are indexed if they appear more than once. A detailed Serra Index follows the General Index.

For contextual perspective, Serra's biography is included, drawn mainly from his own writings, and his legacy is traced from his death to the present. Of the multitude of Serra tributes, from statues and medals to comic books and a World War II Liberty ship, only the history of those commemorating an important site or event in his life are featured, as well as those with national or international significance.

By examining what Serra surrounded himself with in life we not only bring his era alive, but ultimately gain further insight into the very nature of the man himself, prompting us to recall and understand the famous prediction made when he died: *"Non recedet memoria ejus"* (Unfading will be his memory, Sirach 39:9).

Martin J. Morgado
2 January 1991

Junípero Serra's Life and Legacy

Majorca: 1713-1749

Following custom on the Spanish Balearic Island of Majorca, the Serra family of Petra placed a laurel sprig on their front door to announce the birth of a son. Junípero Serra was born at 1 a.m. on Friday 24 November 1713, the third of five children to peasant farmers Antonio Nadal Serra y Abram and Margarita Rosa Ferrer y Fornés, and only one of two who survived infancy.

"As if sensing the great work their new-born son would one day accomplish in baptizing pagans, [Junípero's] devout parents had him baptized on the very day of his birth."[1] He was christened Miguel José Serra y Ferrer at Petra's San Pedro Parish Church. Retaining his baptismal name, Miguel was confirmed on 26 May 1715 by Most Reverend Anastasio Esterripa y Tranajáuregui, Bishop of Majorca. His sponsor was the same priest who officiated at his parent's wedding at San Pedro Church on 7 August 1707, Reverend Pere Mestre.

As soon as Miguel began to walk his parents instructed him "in the rudiments of faith and in the holy fear of God, . . . [and] encouraged him to frequent the nearby *convento* [monastery/school] of Saint Bernardine,"[2] where the Franciscans conducted an elementary school. There he

> studied Latin, learning it perfectly; at the same time he became skillful in plain chant. . . . As a result of these holy exercises and of the devout conversations of his parents, very early in life there took root in his heart fervent desires to wear the holy habit of Our Seraphic Father Saint Francis; but to his regret he was still too young.[3]

At age fifteen, Miguel's parents took him to Palma, the capital of Majorca. There he was entrusted to a canon at the cathedral for three months to assess his vocation. After that he was permitted to enroll in the Franciscan novitiate Convento de Nuestra Señora de los Angeles, where on 14 September 1730 he received the habit of the Observant branch of the mendicant Order of Friars Minor (from the Latin *Fratres Minores*, "Lesser 'Brethren," popularly known as Franciscans, after Saint Francis of Assisi, founder of the Order).

Miguel wore a light blue habit in conformity with the approved custom of the Franciscan Province of Majorca. The wool, ankle-length habit had a cowl (hood) and was held in place by a three-knotted cincture (rope-cord belt). An inner tunic (loose-fitting cotton or wool garment extending to the knees) was worn under the habit. A mantle (wool cape) was worn over the habit in cold weather. Footwear consisted of simple leather or hempen sandals.

Miguel then spent a year in strict seclusion, prayer, study and self-mortification in preparation for his solemn profession into the Order. He enjoyed reading the lives of saints and wished to follow those "who had labored for the conversion of souls. . . . He desired to imitate them even to the point of offering his life and shedding his blood as they had done."[4] He expressed particular devotion to Saint Bernardine of Siena (1380-1444, Italian Franciscan priest), referring to him as "the most special patron of my heart."[5] His devotion to the "Apostle of Italy" was nurtured from early childhood by the Franciscans, along with a deep love for the Virgin Mary, especially under her appellation as the Immaculate Conception. When added to his closeness to Saint Francis Solano (1549-1610, Spanish Franciscan priest known as the "Apostle of South America" and canonized in 1726 when Miguel was thirteen), this completed the triumvirate that was lifelong recipient of his devotion and affection.

Though blessed with a facile memory and strong singing voice, Miguel was hindered by poor health. He wrote: "I was almost always ill and so small of stature that I was unable to reach the lectern, nor could I help my fellow novices in the necessary chores of the novitiate."[6] Only after his profession into the Order at age seventeen on 15 September 1731, did his health and stature improve (he grew to 5 feet, 2 inches and a maximum weight of around 110 pounds). "When[ever] he remembered and spoke of the joy that was his when he made his profession, he broke forth with these words: "All good things came to me together with it"[7] (Wisdom 7:11). At his profession, Miguel knelt in Santa María's sanctuary, and swore the following Latin vow before Very Reverend Antonio Perelló y Moragues, O.F.M., Provincial of the Franciscan Province of Majorca:

> I, Fray Junípero Serra, vow and promise to Almighty God, to the ever Blessed Virgin Mary, to Blessed Father Francis, to all the saints, and to you, Father, to observe for the whole span of my life the rule of the Friars Minor confirmed by His Holiness, Pope Honorius III, by living in obedience, without property and in chastity.[8]

Miguel also chose a new religious name, Junípero, after one of the original companions of Saint Francis of Assisi. Nicknamed the "Jester of God" for his "foolish" simplicity and antics, Blessed Juniper (died 1258) was

> one of the most special first followers of Saint Francis. He was humble and patient . . . and in spite of temptation and troubles he never wavered, in spite of great sufferings no one ever saw him upset. He had such a contempt of self that those who did not know this thought he was stupid or a fool. Saint Francis had this to say about Brother Juniper: "My brothers, my brothers, I wish I had a forest of such junipers."[9]

Junípero transferred to the Franciscan Convento de San Francisco de Palma, and studied philosophy from September 1731 to June 1734. Along with thirty-two other students, he deepened his understanding of divine revelation by delving into logic, ethics, metaphysics and cosmology, all taught in Latin. The method of inquiry was Scholasticism, based on Aristotelian logic as interpreted by John Duns Scotus, founder of the method and medieval *Doctor Subtilis* (Subtle Doctor) of the Franciscan Order. The teachings of the Church Fathers also figured prominently, especially Saint Augustine and Saint Bonaventure. From the writings of Saint Paul, Junípero drew inspiration for his famous motto "*siempre adelante, nunca atrás*" (always [go] forward, never [turn] back).

After completing the philosophy course, Junípero enrolled in San Francisco's three-year theology course. From September 1734 to June 1737 he studied a variety of topics under a number of professors. Among them "the dogma of habitual grace," a "tract on conscience" and a "tract on the angels according to Blessed Ramón Llull," patron of Majorca. On the last page of his final-course notebook, dated 22 June 1737, Junípero wrote: "Today I finished my studies."[10] Nevertheless, he would soon begin studying for a doctorate in Sacred Theology.

In addition to academic studies, Junípero's path to the priesthood consisted of several steps. On 21 December 1731, while a philosophy student, he received tonsure and minor orders from the Bishop of Majorca. Tonsure is shaving the hair from the top of the head, symbolic of Jesus' crown of thorns and a reminder of striving for spiritual perfection. The four minor orders are acolyte, reader, exorcist and doorkeeper.

While studying theology, Junípero was ordained a sub-deacon and a deacon, on 18 December 1734 and 17 March 1736, respectively. The exact date of his ordination to the priesthood is unknown. His name does not appear on the 31 May 1737 record of ordination for his diaconate class because he had not reached the canonically required age of twenty-four. Most likely he was ordained shortly after reaching the proper age on 24 November 1737, and certainly by 21 February 1739, when he received faculties as diocesan confessor from the Bishop of Majorca.

After finishing his studies at Convento de San Francisco, Junípero successfully competed for the *convento's* position of Lector in Philosophy. He received the appointment on 29 November 1737, but served as librarian until the following academic year. From 9 September 1740 to 23 June 1743, he taught San Francisco's complete philosophy course. Among his pupils were Francisco Palóu and Juan Crespí, both natives of Palma who would later accompany him to the New World. On the first day of class he told his students to "walk in [the] light [of knowledge] worthily that you may be sons of Him Who is Light itself and in Whom there is no darkness."[11]

In June 1742, at age twenty-eight, Junípero earned an S.T.D. (Doctor of Sacred Theology) degree from the Pontifical, Imperial, Royal and Literary University of Majorca, commonly known as Llullian University. The topic of his doctoral dissertation and his exact graduation date are unknown.

On 16 October 1743, Junípero was appointed *catedrático de prima* (highest ranking professor) to the Duns Scotus Chair of Sacred Theology at Llullian University. He held the distinguished tenure until his departure for the New World, and was a popular preacher in Palma and various Majorcan towns. After one particularly inspiring sermon, delivered at the invitation of Llullian University professors and benefactors on the 25 January 1749 Feast of Blessed Ramón Llull, it was noted that "[his] sermon is worthy of being printed in letters of gold."[12]

By 1749, when Doctor Serra was thirty-five and "enjoying the high esteem and applause both within and without the Order, . . . the voice of God called him to be a teacher of nations."[13] In his words: "I had no other motive but to revive in my soul those intense longings which I [had] since my novitiate when I read the lives of saints. These longings had become deadened because of the preoccupation I had with studies."[14] On feeling his reawakened call, Junípero "had recourse to God in prayer, choosing as his intercessors God's Most Pure Mother and Saint Francis Solano, Apostle of the Indies."[15] He did not share his intention to become a New World apostolic missionary *de Propaganda Fide* (for the Propagation of the Faith) with anyone at first,

3

but prayed that his intercessors would "bestir the heart of someone to go with [him]."[16] When he learned that former student Francisco Palóu had independently reached the same decision, he "shed tears" and said: "It is, without doubt, God's will."[17]

While waiting for the necessary exit documents, Junípero preached the Lenten course at Petra's San Pedro Church from Ash Wednesday 19 February to Easter Sunday 6 April 1749. Then,

> after preaching the last sermon in the same parish church where he had been baptized, and having bade farewell to his countrymen, but without disclosing [that he was going to Mexico], he left Petra on Easter Tuesday to return to the friary in the city [of Palma]. This he did after he had visited his aged parents and after he had bade them [his customary] farewell and received their blessing, his local task being finished. He left [his parents] in ignorance of his [ultimate] plans, for this reason acting all the more in secret.[18]

Junípero's farewell at Palma's Convento de San Francisco was

> one of tears rather than of words. Naturally the very deeply affected community was touched with emotion at this scene, when it saw the Reverend Father Junípero going about at the very last kissing the feet of all the friars even down to the lowest novice.[19]

On 13 April 1749, Junípero and Francisco sailed from Palma to Málaga and Cádiz, the first leg of their 5,000-mile sea journey to Mexico, capital of New Spain. En route, the anti-clerical English skipper

> continually wanted to argue or dispute on dogmas. . . . [Although they] never started a conversation or an argument with him, . . . he threatened to throw [them] overboard, . . . and one night, . . . placed a dagger at [Junípero's] throat apparently with the intention of taking his life. . . . [He eventually relented], and during the rest of the journey he was not so annoying.[20]

Cádiz Board of Trade officials documented all missionaries who passed through and Junípero was recorded as "lector of theology, native of Petra in the Diocese of Majorca, thirty-five years old, of medium height, swarthy, dark eyes and hair, scant beard"[21] (this is the only known, contemporaneous physical description of Junípero). From Cádiz, Junípero wrote to one of Petra's San Bernardino Franciscans, asking him to convey his decision to leave to his parents, who were illiterate. He wrote in part:

> I wish I could give them some of the happiness that is mine; and I feel that they would urge me to go ahead and never to turn back. . . . The remainder [of their lives] is short, and should they compare it with eternity, they will see that it is no more than an instant. If this be so, it is very important, and according to God's will, that they lay no store by the little help I might be to them [if I stayed]. And

so they will merit from God, Our Lord, that if we are no more to see each other in this world, we will be united forever in eternal glory. . . . They will find how sweet His yoke can be, that what they consider and endure as a great sorrow will be turned into a lasting joy. Nothing in this life should cause us sadness. Our clear duty is to conform ourselves in all things to the will of God, and to prepare to die well. That is what counts; nothing else matters. . . . May the Lord bring us all together in eternal glory, . . . that is my prayer.[22]

Junípero never saw his parents again. His father died four years later at age 77, and his mother one year after that, also at age 77.

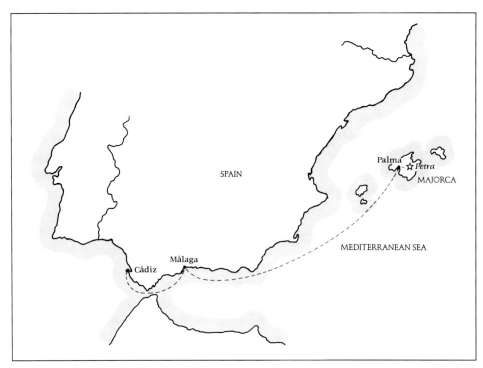

1. Serra's Majorcan travels: 1713-1749.

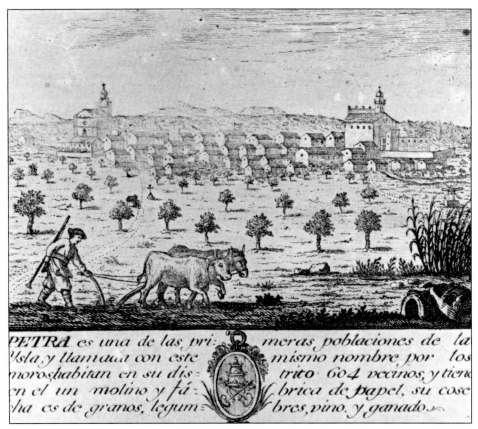

PETRA es una de las pri=   meras poblaciones de la
Ysla, y llamaaa con este   mísmo nombre por los
moros,habitan en su dis=   trito 604 vecinos, y tien
en el un molino y fá=   brica de papel, su cose
ha es de granos, legum=   bres, vino, y ganados

2. Petra, Majorca, Spain (population 2,000 in Serra's day). Detail from a 1785 map, showing San Pedro Parish Church on the left and San Bernardino Franciscan Church on the right. The legend translates: "Petra is one of the first towns of the island, and called with this same name by the Moorish. Six hundred and four residents inhabit this district [reduced from Serra's day by epidemic/drought], and it has a windmill and paper factory. Its harvest is of grains, vegetables, wine and livestock." The Papal tiara and crossed keys, adopted as the municipal coat of arms after King James I of Aragon wrested the Balearic Islands from the Moors in 1229, refers to Petra's etymology: Petra is Latin for "rock" and as Jesus said to the first Pope, "Thou art Peter and upon this rock I will build my church" (Matthew 16:19).

3. Modern Petra (population 3,000) from Bon Any Hill. In the background, the mountains that ring the 1400-square-mile island, and the Bay of Alcudia on the Mediterranean Sea, from where the ancient Greeks, Phoenicians and Romans first entered Majorca.

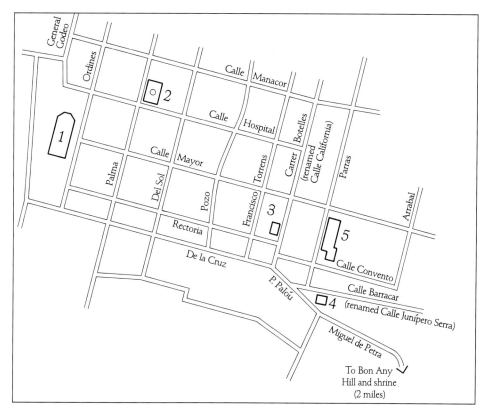

4. Petra's Serra landmarks: (1) San Pedro Parish Church; (2) Plaza de Junípero Serra, and Serra statue erected in 1913; (3) site of Serra's *casa natal* (birth house); (4) Serra's *casa solariega* (ancestral or boyhood house); (5) San Bernardino Franciscan Church/former *convento*.

5. *Casa natal* (left structure) at 48 Carrer Botelles, Petra, where Serra was born. The house, belonging to his maternal grandmother (established by her will, which is preserved in the Diocese of Majorca Archives), was where the Serra family lived until 1719, when Serra was six. The building remained in the family until 1839, when the last direct descendant died (Serra's grandnephew through his sister Juana). Demolished in 1930, the unmarked site is now occupied by two new dwellings at 46-48 Calle California.

6. San Pedro Parish Church, where Serra was baptized and confirmed. Named after Saint Peter the Apostle, the cornerstone was laid on 30 May 1582. Built gradually of local Santanyi stone, the Late Gothic structure was dedicated on 15 October 1730, although not completed until 1766. (Calle Ordines, Petra)

7. San Pedro interior. Serra saw the last phase of construction before leaving Majorca in 1749, and was familiar with most of the interior and furnishings. The Neoclassic *reredos* (altarpiece) with statue of Saint Peter is a nineteenth-century addition. Serra's baptismal font is on the Gospel side of the sanctuary, and next to it a statue of Saint Praxedes, patroness of Petra.

8. San Pedro's original sandstone baptismal font where Serra was baptized, with Petra's coat of arms sculpted on its octagonal sides. At some point during the nineteenth century, it was replaced by a new font and retired to the rectory garden. There it "served as a flowerpot for many years"[23] until being returned to the church, circa 1930. It was moved to the sanctuary in 1984. 36" tall x 29" bowl diameter.

9. Baptismal font detail. Serra's font is still in use today, as well as the eighteenth-century silver baptismal shell, which may be the one used to baptize him.

10. Serra's baptismal record. Listed in San Pedro's *Libro de Bautismos* (*Book of Baptisms*), volume II, verso 63, entry number 85, it is written in Mallorquín, a dialect of Catalan spoken in Majorca. Translation: "Miquel Joseph Serre. On 24 November 1713, I Bartolomé Lledó, priest and vicar, baptized Miquel Joseph Serre, son of Antoni and Margarita Ferrer, married. The sponsors were Bartolomé Fiol and Sebastiana Serre. He was born on the same day, at one [hour] after midnight." Miguel is spelled Miquel in Mallorquín, and Serra is Serre. Sebastiana was a paternal aunt, Bartolomé a maternal relative. Reverend Francisco Torrens y Nicolau, early twentieth-century Serra historian, added the cross and Spanish inscription. Translation: "Today he is the Venerable Father Fray Junípero Serra, Apostle of California. He died in Monterey on 28 August 1784. F[rancisco] T[orrens]." (San Pedro Church sacristy, Petra)

11. *Casa solariega* at 6 Calle Barracar Alta (now Calle California), Petra, where Serra lived from age six to fifteen. His father received the land as a gift from his brother Miguel in 1718, and commenced to build a house and corral. The deed of transfer, preserved in Palma's Archivo del Reino de Mallorca, is dated 29 October 1719. Serra, his parents and younger sister Juana moved in shortly thereafter, but there is no firsthand account of the years spent there. The house passed from the Serra family in 1839, and fell into disrepair. In 1932, the Rotary Club of Majorca purchased and restored it, and established the Serra Casa Solariega and Museum. Legal title was presented to the city of San Francisco, California as "a solid fraternal link between [the] country in which Serra was born, and the country in which he discharged his missionary labors."[24] The property was maintained by Petra's "sister-city" and the

Society of California Pioneers until budget considerations prompted San Francisco's Board of Supervisors to return title in 1980. The two-story, stone and tile-roofed structure has a frontage of twenty-eight feet. The property line begins where the stone façade changes texture (immediately to the left of the square mulecart storage-room door) and extends slightly past the arched main entrance to a point where the stone again changes texture. The Spanish plaque translates: "Ancestral home of Venerable Father Fray Junípero Serra, O.F.M., Apostle of California 1713-1784. The town and people of Petra."

12. *Casa solariega* interior. The main living area measures 14'8" x 17'8" and is furnished with period pieces, although none belonged to the Serra family. In 1932, the California Historical Society publicly appealed for "suitable historical relics of the Spanish period in California. Each gift . . . was examined carefully to establish its authenticity and suitability. Before long there were more gifts than could be placed in the little house."[25] The cobblestone path leads down a short hallway to a small kitchen-alcove on the left with open hearth and chimney, a bedroom-alcove, and on the right, an indoor mule stable. The enclosed backyard served as corral, henhouse, garden, and had a bakeoven and woodshed. The second story, reached via staircase from the main room, contains a small bedroom used by Serra's parents and a storage area. Two shuttered windows admit light and air.

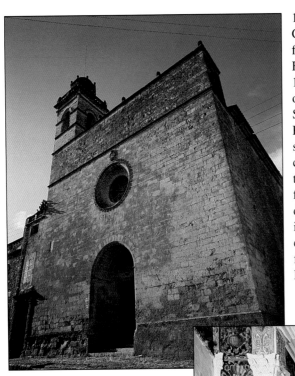

13. San Bernardino Franciscan Church, only a few hundred yards from Serra's *casa solariega*. The Franciscans first came to Petra in 1607, and soon began construction of a church/*convento*. Named after Saint Bernardine of Siena, the Late Renaissance, Santanyi stone structure was dedicated in 1672 and completed in 1677. Serra attended the *convento's* elementary school from age six to fifteen, and passed daily through its entrance immediately to the left of the church, now the only vestige of the former *convento*. (Calle Convento, Petra)

14. San Bernardino interior. The Baroque *reredos* dates from 1679 and features the Immaculate Conception, installed when Serra was eight. Saint John Capistran is on the left and Saint James of the Marches on the right. Saint Bernardine occupies the uppermost niche. The left murals depict the Theological Virtues Faith, Hope and Charity, and the right ones the Religious Virtues Obedience, Poverty and Humility. Serra's parents, sister Juana and her husband Miguel are buried in the aisle crypt, inscribed in Mallorquín: "Sepulcher for the members and devotees of the Immaculate Conception, 1744." Members of this confraternity paid for special church projects and maintenance, and were accorded the privilege of burial within.

15. Detail from a 1644 map of Palma, Majorca, showing Palma Cathedral (bottom arrow); Llullian University (middle); and Church/Convento de San Francisco (upper right). The Majorcan capital, twenty-five miles from Petra (a seven-hour trip at that time), has grown from 50,000 in Serra's day to 500,000 today.

16. Ruins of the Convento de Nuestra Señora de los Angeles (Our Lady of the Angels), where Serra lived during his novitiate year. Founded in 1441, the *convento* was located *extramuros* or just "outside" Palma's medieval walls, within a pine forest. The church/*convento* complex was destroyed after Majorcan secularization of church property in 1835, and all that remains is a 55-foot section of the double-arched Gothic cloister. (Avenida Esporla, Palma)

17. Cloister of the Convento de San Francisco de Palma, where Serra lived from September 1731 to April 1749. The Franciscans first came to Majorca in 1232, only six years after Saint Francis of Assisi's death, and settled at this site in 1278. The three-story, fourteenth-century cloister, the "flower of Majorcan Gothic art," is a Spanish national monument. The functioning well in the center is inscribed 1658. San Francisco originally consisted of two cloisters, but only one remains with its interior now remodeled as an elementary school. Therefore, it is impossible to locate exactly where Serra lived, studied and taught, but this is still the most complete Serra "shrine," *el alma* (the soul) of his early adulthood. (Plaza de San Francisco, Palma)

18. Serra's signature with official *rubrica* (rubric, from the Spanish *rubricar*, to sign and seal). Spanish schoolboys designed and perfected highly individualized flourishes at the end of their signatures, a legal requirement akin to a seal or official stamp. Even though Serra became a priest, he chose to follow the Spanish Franciscan custom of preceding his name with *Fray* (from the Latin *Frater*, Brother) rather than *Padre* (Father), out of humility.

19. Detail from the final page of one of Serra's Latin philosophy notebooks, written at age eighteen. The final paragraph translates: "And these words will suffice, for the undertaken work satisfies my promise to you [his professor], and let all be for the honor and praise of the Most Holy Trinity, *viz.*, of the unbegotten Father, the only-begotten Son, and the Holy Spirit from either preceding, and of the Most Pure Ever Virgin Mary shining in original splendor, of Our Seraphic Father Saint Francis, Anthony of Padua, Seraphic Doctor Bonaventure, Bernardine of Siena, the most special patron of my heart, and also Our Venerable Teacher and Most Sublime Doctor John Duns Scotus, and of all the citizens of Heaven, whose merits humbly and incessantly I implore, so that, just as we finish the small logic, so [may we finish] the great, by the grace of God,

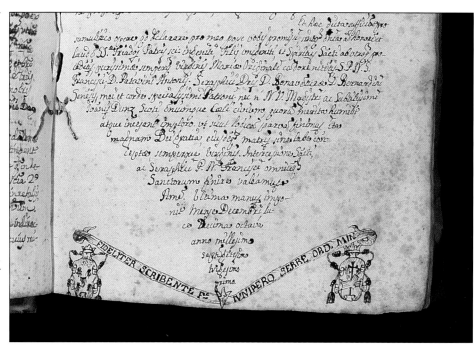

and of His same mother without stain, conceived and ever Virgin. By the intercession of Saint and Seraphic Saint Francis and of all the saints we have the strength to finish. Amen. The last stroke I put in the month of December on the eighteenth day in the year one thousand seven hundred thirty one." Serra's scroll translates: "With Friar Junípero Serra of the Minor Order faithfully writing." On the left, he drew the *Cinco Llagas* (Five Wounds) of the Crucifixion, depicted as five hearts, a popular symbol in Franciscan art. On the right, the First Order Franciscan coat of arms, composed of the arms of Jesus and Saint Francis of Assisi in saltire, both with stigmata and surmounted by a cross. (Manuscript 882, page 50, Archivo del Estado, Majorca Public Library, Palma)

20. Serra's diagram of a Ptolemaic universe with the sun and planets revolving around a geocentric earth. Made from superimposed disks of paper, the handmade chart is delicately fastened to his notebook page, allowing each disk to rotate individually. (Manuscript 882, page 259, Archivo del Estado, Majorca Public Library, Palma)

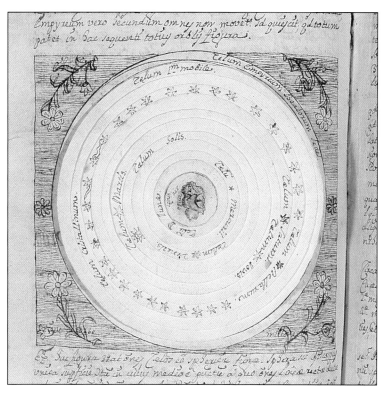

21. San Francisco Church (a minor basilica since 1943), adjoining the Convento de San Francisco. Named after Saint Francis of Assisi (1181-1226, Italian founder of the Order of Friars Minor in 1210), the cornerstone was laid on 31 January 1281 by King James II of Aragon. The Gothic structure, built of Santanyi stone, has a Baroque seventeenth-century façade designed by noted Spanish architect Francisco de Herrera. The Immaculate Conception adorns the portal's central niche, with Blessed Ramón Llull on the left and John Duns Scotus on the right. Below them, Saint Dominic (left) and Saint Francis of Assisi (right). Above the portal, Saint George, and on the uppermost towers, Saint Peter of Alcántara (left) and Saint Peter Baptist (right). The bronze statue of Serra and Indian boy, commissioned by the city of Palma and sculpted by Horacio de Eguía, was dedicated in 1976. (Plaza de San Francisco, Palma)

22. San Francisco interior, Serra's "home" church for almost eighteen years. The basilica, second-largest in Majorca after the cathedral, has a nave measuring 243 feet long by 46 wide by 82 high. The Baroque main altar was installed during a 1732-39 remodeling, and Serra delivered the dedication sermon on 29 October 1739. Saint Francis of Assisi occupies the central niche above the tabernacle, and at the same level on the right, Saint Bonaventure, Saint Catherine of Bologna and Saint Roch. On the left, Saint Anthony of Padua, Saint Clare and Saint Louis IX, King of France. Saint Dominic is to the left of the tabernacle, Blessed Ramón Llull to the right, and the Immaculate Conception above it. Saint George crowns the *reredos*.

23. San Francisco's pulpit, where Serra preached on many occasions, including when it was said that his words were "worthy of being printed in letters of gold." He also preached his final Majorcan sermon here, on 10 April 1749.

24. San Francisco's sacristy. Several furnishings date from Serra's tenure, including the vestment cases, art work, statues and some of the sacred vessels and vestments. Two chalices, a silver reliquary with *Lingum Crucis* (True Cross relic), a silver incense boat and a silver reliquary containing Blessed Ramón Llull's mandible are displayed on the vestment case. The open choirbook is similar to the one Serra was too short to reach at Nuestra Señora de los Angeles novitiate.

25. Alabaster sepulcher of Blessed Ramón Llull in San Francisco Basilica. Historically revered by the Franciscans as *Doctor Illuminatus* (Illuminated Doctor), Palma's university was named in his honor and his writings influenced Franciscan thought through Serra's day. Llull (known as Raymond Lull or Lully in English) was born in Palma in 1235. After a series of mystical visions on Majorca's Mount Randa, he joined the Franciscan Secular Order. He traveled throughout North Africa and Asia Minor converting Moors, and according to legend was stoned to death in Algeria in 1315. Llull's major work, *Ars Generalis Ultima* (*Highest General Knowledge*, circa 1308), was a theosophical attempt to encompass all knowledge into a Neoplatonic schema that resolved all religious differences. He also composed religious poetry, mystical literature, an encyclopedia of medieval thought, and approximately 250 philosophical and theological treatises in Latin, Arabic and Catalan. Those addressing the *cultus* (cult) of the Blessed Virgin Mary, along with the writings of John Duns Scotus, paved the way for the modern Catholic dogmas of the Immaculate Conception and the Assumption.

26. Serra's woodblock for imprinting holy cards of Blessed Juniper, his religious namesake. The woodblock, made of local *boj* wood, was inked and pressed on paper to make "holy cards" for distribution to the faithful. Juniper wears a Franciscan habit and halo, holds a lily of purity, and his outstretched right hand invokes God's intercession. The *Manus Dei* (Hand of God) is breaking through the clouds as per a vision when Juniper was praying, and a voice utters in Latin: "A hand without a hand can do nothing." The juniper bush recalls Saint Francis' wish for a "forest" of junipers. The two demons and tower refer to an encounter Juniper had with a "certain very cruel ruler named Nicholas, who was in charge of a fortress."[26] The devil prodded him to harm Juniper, because "proud devils" could not stand his "humility and innocence." Juniper was placed on a rack, dragged by a horse through the city and then almost hanged. There is another demon in the tower pushing the man in front of him (possibly Nicholas being tempted), and he in turn pushing three other men (Juniper was also "roughed up by a gang of wild young men" on the same occasion). The Latin legend translates: "Blessed Juniper one of the first disciples of Our Holy Father Francis [of Assisi]." Serra's carved Spanish inscription on the woodblock's reverse side (not shown here) translates: "This belongs to [for the use of] Father lector Junípero. 1741." 5-7/8" x 3-5/8" thick. (San Francisco Church sacristy, Palma)

27. Detail from the first page of one of Serra's sermons. Of all the sermons he preached only four survive, all written in his own hand. Composed in 1744, they were delivered as a Lenten series to the Franciscan Poor Clare Nuns at Palma's Convento de Santa Clara, and entitled: "On the Gentleness of God in His Divine Callings;" On the Softness of God in His Holy Law;" On the Softness of the Lord, Even in the Sufferings He Sends Us;" and "On the Softness of the Lord in His Mercy." The twenty-seven Mallorquín, Spanish, and Latin pages touch upon a number of scriptural themes and quote

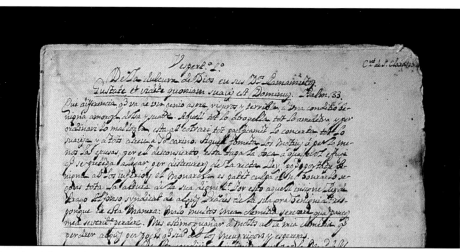

from the Old and New Testaments, the writings and lives of various Church Fathers, and the Saints. Serra brought the sermons to Mexico in 1749, where they remained until being returned to Majorca in the early nineteenth-century. Translation of the first paragraph: "First Evening Sermon. On the Gentleness of God in His Divine Callings. Taste and see that the Lord is sweet, Psalm 33. What a difference there is between a gruff, harsh and terrible temperament, and a benign, loving, sweet and gentle character. The former tramples down, intimidates and usually ruins everything. Generally, the latter peacefully makes harmony and mollifies everything, and attracts everybody to its love. The former fosters the motives or at least the excuses for disharmony, the latter represses any subterfuge that seeks to be close in order to distract us from the true law, and considers that, when the king behaves benignly toward his subjects, one suffers guilt for not honoring him according to the stature of his dignity. This good nature was manifested by that renowned King of Aragon, Alfonso, when some of the grandees thought that his indulgence was too great. His answer to them was: "I prefer to win over many with my mercy, than to lose some, no matter how few, with my severity and harshness." (Convento de San Francisco Archives, Palma)

28. Llullian University, where Serra received his doctorate in Sacred Theology. Founded in 1483, it was originally called Estudio General Llulliano (Llullian General Study). The name was changed to Imperial and Royal University after Charles I of Spain granted university status in 1526, and to its full title of Pontifical, Imperial, Royal and Literary University of Majorca after receiving papal approbation in 1673. Operating at its peak in Serra's day, the university maintained schools of theology, law and medicine. Closed from 1832-1951 due to declining enrollment, and its buildings demolished, it now operates in new buildings on the same site as a semiautonomous branch of the University of Barcelona. The carving over the door is the only original remnant, with the Majorcan, Spanish and Llull family coats of arms. On the opposing wall, the Blessed Virgin Mary and Child Jesus are attended by Llull and Serra. (Calle Estudio General and San Roque, Palma)

29. Palma Cathedral, where Serra preached on three occasions. The massive Gothic structure, built over the course of the thirteenth through sixteenth centuries, sits on a bluff overlooking the Bay of Palma. When Serra sailed from his homeland in 1749, it was the last landmark to fade from view. (Plaza de la Almoina, Palma)

30. Cathedral interior, where Serra delivered the prestigious annual Feast of Corpus Christi sermon on 13 June 1743. As recorded in the Convento de San Francisco's *Libro de Gastos y Entradas* (*Book of Expenses and Earnings*), his topic was the Holy Eucharist. He received an honorarium, but all "alms" were paid directly to the *convento's* intermediary syndic, in conformity with the Franciscan rule against individual handling of money. The cathedral interior, with fourteen columns supporting three lofty vaults, measures 400 feet long by 55 wide by 145 high. Twenty-one side chapels adorn the nave and two Aragonese kings lie buried within. The main altar was remodeled in the nineteenth century by noted Spanish architect Antoni Gaudí.

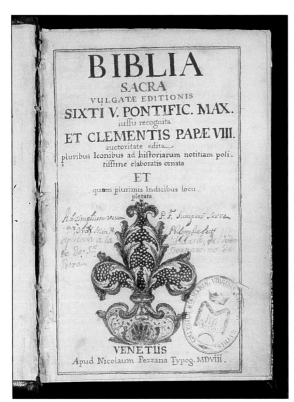

31. Title page of Serra's Bible, the only one found to date with his signature. His Latin inscription translates: "For the simple use of Father Fray Junípero Serra, of the Order of Friars Minor, Philosophy Lector." The Spanish inscription below his reads: "From the library of the Convento de San Bernardino de Petra." The Bible was rebound in leather-covered pasteboard and the first two pages, including the title page, were recopied. This was done by the *convento's* calligrapher, shortly before, or while Serra was using it. He left the Bible behind when departing Majorca for Mexico, most likely donating it to the *convento* at that time. The Latin title-page translates: "The Holy Bible of the Vulgate Edition. Revised at the order of the Supreme Pontiff Sixtus V and published under the authority of Pope Clement VIII. Adorned with many illustrations produced most exquisitely with regard to the concept of the narrative and enriched with as many indexes as possible. At Venice: Nicolaus Pezzana Publishing, 1508 [*sic*] [Sixtus died in 1590, Clement in 1605. An error was made when recopying the title page, which should read 1608]." 1,170 pages. 6-5/16" x 4-3/4" x 2-3/8" thick. (Diocese of Majorca Colegio de Sapiencia Archives, Palma)

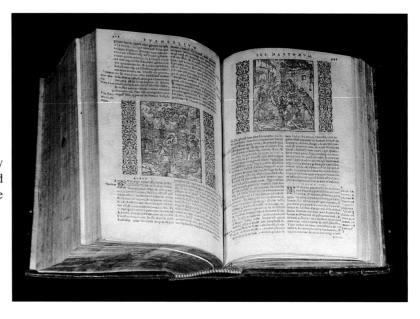

32. Two etchings from Serra's profusely illustrated Bible. The Nativity is depicted on the left and the Presentation on the right.

33. Title page of Serra's Biblical concordance. A concordance is an alphabetical index of key words and phrases with a reference to the passage in which each can be found. Serra also left this book behind in Majorca, as the Mallorquín inscription on the half-title page attests (not shown, and not in Serra's hand): "These concordances were applied by the Reverend Father Fray Junípero Serra from Petra to the common library of the Convento de San Bernardino from that said town, the same year that he left Majorca for Mexico, having been appointed Apostolic Missionary *de Propaganda Fide*, the said year 1749." Early in this century, the concordance was purchased by a California collector, rebound in fine leather, and held privately. On 16 September 1987, the Archdiocese of Los Angeles, which had acquired the book, presented it to Pope John Paul II on the occasion of his second pastoral visit to the United States. Serra's Latin inscription translates: "For the simple use of Fray Junípero Serra, Observant Order of Friars Minor." The Latin title-page translates: "Concordance of the Vulgate Edition of the Holy Bible of Cardinal Hugo of the Order of Preachers. Revised and emended with respect to the revision made to the Bible at the order of the Supreme Pontiff Sixtus V, first by Francis Luca, Theologian and Deacon of Saint-Omer, now again amended in various places and enriched by the care and diligence of V.D. Hubert Phalesius, Order of Saint Benedict. Venice, 1733. At [the office of] Nicolaus Pezzana, by permission of Superiors, and by privilege." 1,028 pages. 12" x 8-1/2" x 3-3/4" thick. (Reserve of Precious Books, number I63, Vatican Library)

Ntra Sra de Bonañy

34. Nuestra Señora de Bon Any (Our Lady of the Good Year). Before leaving his hometown for the last time in April 1749, Serra made a final pilgrimage to the hilltop shrine of Nuestra Señora de Bon Any, probably on 1 April, the feast of the Virgin. The hill is located two miles southwest of Petra and rises 500 feet above it, or 1,289 feet above sea level. According to local tradition, severe sixteenth-century droughts were ended by city-wide novenas and a pilgrimage to the hill. Hence the title, the shrine (completed in 1609, replaced in 1789 and again in 1925) and the following prayer of thanksgiving: "Give us a good year, O Lady, for key to a good year thou art."[27] The sixteenth-century, refinished statue of the Virgin Mary and Child Jesus remained in Serra's thoughts after he left Majorca. On 3 September 1782, he recorded the following in Mission San Carlos Borromeo's *Libro de Bautismos*: "I solemnly baptized a girl about thirteen years old, the daughter of pagans, and gave her the name María de Buen Año. This is the title by which Most Holy Mary is known in my beloved homeland."[28] 24" tall. (Bon Any Shrine, Petra)

Mexico: 1749-1769

Junípero's transatlantic voyage lasted from 29 August to 18 October 1749. After arriving in San Juan, Puerto Rico, he performed his first missionary work by directing a two-week "mission" of religious services and preaching among the local citizenry.

During the five-week voyage to the Mexican mainland, during which Junípero was the only one "who did not get seasick," the ship was temporarily blown off course by a violent storm that threatened shipwreck. During the storm, in which "the ship was filling with water" and "the mainmast continued in use only by a miracle," each of the twenty Franciscan and seven Dominican priests on board put the name of their favorite saint in a bowl, so that

> by drawing lots, [we] would know who would be our special patron and protector.
> . . . In honor of the one elected, we agreed, all would have to assist at a solemn
> Mass and sermon when safe on land. I [Junípero] wrote down Saint Francis
> Solano, but [he] did not win. Saint Barbara did . . . and it turned out that on her
> feast day, December 4, at night, the ship sailed back towards port, and we all felt
> happy and confident."[29]

On Sunday 7 December 1749, Junípero first stepped ashore on continental North America at Vera Cruz, Mexico. As a spiritual exercise, he chose to walk the 275-mile tropical stretch of El Camino Real to Mexico City's San Fernando Apostolic College *de Propaganda Fide*. Along the way, mosquito or chigger bites infected his lower left leg. Recurrent inflammations, eventually developing into an ulcerated, possibly cancerous growth, would afflict him for the rest of his life. He sought no medical care, choosing to leave such matters "in the hands of the Divine Physician."[30]

Upon entering Mexico City, Junípero stopped to say Mass at the Basilica of Our Lady of Guadalupe on New Year's Day 1750. He then proceeded to San Fernando College. This was not an educational institution in the traditional sense, but rather a missionary recruitment, fieldwork training and administrative center for the Franciscan Order.

Once at San Fernando, Junípero exchanged his blue habit for the college's ash gray one, woven from undyed black and white wool (provincial distinctions were abolished in 1897, and most Franciscans now wear brown). Denied a request to repeat his novitiate year as an act of humility, Junípero instead spent the next five months in intensive missionary preparation for his first fieldwork assignment. Following his typical routine, he performed many humble acts for his confreres, slept little, avoided meat for sparse portions of fish, vegetables and fruit, and fasted frequently.

Consistent with Spain's Counter Reformation religious *Zeitgeist*, Junípero practiced self-mortification as a "daily death" of the flesh in mystic union with the Passion of Christ and as an act of penance for his sins and the sins of others. Junípero

> was not content with the ordinary exercises of [San Fernando] in regard to acts
> of discipline, vigils and fasts. He privately scourged his flesh with rough hair
> shirts, made either of bristles or with points of metal wire, with which he covered

his body. He also took the *disciplina* [an iron and braided-wire scourge] unto blood during the most silent part of the night. . . . He also did [public] penance for the sins of others. By strong censures he would move his listeners [from the pulpit] to sorrow and penance for their sins; he struck his breast with the stone, in imitation of Saint Jerome; in imitation of Saint Francis Solano, to whom he was devoted, he used the chain to scourge himself; he used the burning torch [candle], applying it to his uncovered chest, burning his flesh in imitation of Saint John Capistran and various other saints.[31]

As San Fernando College's *Método de Misionar* (*Missionary Methods*, published 1780) handbook suggests, self-mortification, at least publicly, was waning by the late-eighteenth century:

Some missionaries have the custom of taking out a chain, and, uncovering their shoulders, scourging themselves with it while they ask the Lord for mercy. . . . Although this is a most efficacious means to move and to break hard hearts, great modesty, prudence and judgment are needed to use it. And although Saint Francis Solano used this means, and other illustrious missionaries have done likewise, it was only on rare occasions; so our missionaries must not make it ordinary and commonplace.[32]

Junípero's missionary career began in the rugged, mountainous Sierra Gorda region of Mexico, located 8,000 feet above sea level. He spent eight years (1750-58) among the Pame Indians of the Chichimeca ethnic and Otomi linguistic group, who lived in settlements of approximately 800 each at five previously established missions spaced roughly fifteen miles apart. He served as administrative *padre presidente* (father president) of the chain from 1751 to 1755, and resided at centrally-located Jalpan, the capital.

Upon his arrival at Jalpan with Francisco Palóu after a sixteen-day, 175-mile walk north from Mexico City, Junípero quickly mastered the difficult Pame language, composed a native catechism, and attracted and instructed the Indians with a visual method of teaching. For example, to encourage frequent Confession he quietly confessed to Francisco in the church sanctuary, in full view of the congregation. In contrast to his personal simplicity, Junípero sought the best possible furnishings for the mission churches. Beautiful sacred vessels, altar linens, candlesticks, statues and paintings allowed him to share his faith with the Indians in a manner that evoked the power and splendor of Christianity.

Junípero also improved agricultural and farming methods by introducing new tools, communal planting and harvesting, and several stock animals. With his help the Indians became "skilled in various trades as stonemasons, carpenters, ironworkers, painters, gilders, etc., [and the women] in spinning, weaving, making stockings, knitting, sewing, etc."[33] He helped them build a new stone church and did not "disdain to perform the most menial and humble chores, working as a day laborer or as a helper to the artisan in carrying stones to build [Santiago de Jalpan Church]."[34]

Although claiming "he did not know how to sing the scales well enough to be of any help,"[35] Junípero was fond of music, and used song and hymn to inspire the Indians. He choreographed a Nativity play for Indian children and often reenacted the events of religious holidays with paraliturgical presentations. During Lent he carried a cross on his shoulder at outdoor Stations of the Cross processions, "so large and heavy that I [Francisco], stronger and younger though I was, could not lift it."[36] On Good Friday he washed the feet of twelve elderly men in imitation of Jesus at the Last Supper. That afternoon the Deposition Ceremony reenacted Jesus being lowered from the Cross. On Easter Sunday, "very early in the morning, the procession of the Risen Christ was held."[37] He always

> used every means and method that his apostolic zeal suggested . . . [to] instill in the neophytes [newly-baptized Indians, as opposed to unbaptized "gentiles" or "pagans"] a great and tender devotion . . . [to] Our Lord, the Most Holy Virgin, . . . to the Most Holy Patriarch Saint Joseph, to Our Seraphic Father Saint Francis and to [all the] saints.[38]

Junípero left Jalpan for the last time in mid-September 1758, returning to San Fernando College to prepare for a new assignment at Mission San Sabá de la Santa Cruz (present Menard County, central Texas). Francisco and he were slated to replace two missionaries recently killed by Comanche Indians, about which Junípero wrote to his nephew in Majorca: "I am quite conscious of my uselessness . . . for so great an enterprise. However, God is strong enough to accomplish out of nothing works which redound to his great glory."[39] Before their departure, the viceroy declared the volatile area off limits until peace could be restored. The viceroy died, the assignment was never reinstated, and Junípero spent the next nine years as a San Fernando "home" missionary in Mexico City.

Junípero served as college counselor, master of novices, choir director and confessor within San Fernando. Also, as apostolic preacher, confessor, and commissary of the Holy Office of the Inquisition throughout the Archdiocese of Mexico and the surrounding dioceses of Oaxaca, Morelia, Puebla and Guadalajara.

During one of his preaching assignments in a remote region east of the Sierra Gorda, Junípero's life was threatened when he drank tainted altar wine during Mass. After nearly collapsing, he was escorted from the altar to a bed in the sacristy. He refused a purgative, but took a sip of oil to calm his stomach. When he regained speech, his first words were: "*Si mortiferum quid biberint, non eis nocebit*"[40] (They will be able to drink deadly poison without harm, Mark 16:18). No one knows who tampered with the wine or why, but Junípero did explain why he refused the remedy:

> It was not . . . because I disbelieved in its effectiveness, nor because I had any horror of it, for in other circumstances I would have taken it. But I had just received the Bread of Angels, which by the power of consecration ceased to be bread and was changed into the body of my Lord Jesus Christ. . . . How could you ask me to take so nauseating a drink, after tasting the Divine Morsel?[41]

Junípero survived ten "brushes with death" during the course of his life, and felt he was assisted by Divine Providence on a number of occasions. Once while traveling in Mexico he was helped by a "well dressed and courteous man" who offered food and shelter during a night "covered with ice owing to the cold rain." He believed him to be Saint Joseph or at least "a devout man whose heart this saint touched to do these acts of charity."[42] On another occasion in Mexico, Junípero and a fellow missionary were offered shelter by a "venerable man with his wife and child." The next day they learned there was no one living in the area, in fact no "house or ranch for many leagues." Junípero believed

> it had been Divine Providence which had granted them the favor of that hospitality, and that undoubtedly those persons who were within the house were Jesus, Mary and Joseph. They pondered not only the neatness and cleanliness of the house, despite its poverty, and the affectionate tenderness with which they dispensed their hospitality, but also on the extraordinary inner consolation which they had felt in their hearts. They gave God Our Lord the thanks he deserved for the special favor they had received.[43]

In July 1767, Junípero was transferred to the coastal town of Loreto, capital of Baja or "Lower" California, located 250 miles north of the peninsula's tip. There he served as newly-appointed *presidente* of the peninsula's previously established fifteen missions. Within a year he learned of the Spanish Crown's forthcoming temporal and spiritual colonization of Alta or "Upper" California north of the thirtieth parallel, and enthusiastically volunteered for the "Sacred Expedition . . . to erect the holy standard of the cross in Monterey"[44] (known through previous explorer's records). He was appointed *presidente* of the future missions, and spent the next three months touring the Lower California missions to recruit volunteers and collect church furnishings. Five separate contingents, three by sea and two by land, were organized to carry settlers and supplies to the new territory.

Accompanied by two guards and an attendant, Junípero began the 95-day, 750-mile journey north from Loreto to San Diego Bay on 28 March 1769. Averaging four hours travel per day on muleback, the small band traveled alone for the first half of the march until joining Military Governor Gaspar de Portolá and the second land contingent at Mission Santa María de los Angeles.

Junípero kept a detailed diary of the entire journey and rated potential mission sites according to availability of water, wood and proximity to Indians. En route on 1 April, he visited Francisco Palóu (replacement *presidente* of the Lower California missions) at Mission San Francisco Xavier, and Francisco, thinking he would never see Junípero again, said farewell "until we meet in eternity."[45] A more prescient Junípero bade him good-bye "until we meet in Monterey, where I hope we shall see each other in order to labor in the vineyard of the Lord."[46]

On 13 May, Junípero reached a long, narrow, river-fed valley called Velicatá, meaning "place of the reeds" to the local Indians of the Yuman ethnic and Cochimí linguistic group. With permission previously granted by San Fernando College, he decided to establish a mission settlement, thereby shortening the gap between the Lower California missions and the intended location of the first Upper California mission at San Diego, 300 miles north.

On Pentecost Sunday 14 May, Junípero constructed an *enramada* (brush-hut shelter) at the site, said Mass, and gave a "fervent talk on the descent of the Holy Spirit and on the founding of the mission."[47] Afterward, "with all the surroundings of holy poverty" he raised and blessed a cross to establish his first Indian mission. He named it San Fernando, after the patron saint of his apostolic college. He left the mission under the care of another missionary and continued northward, never to return.

A couple of days later, Junípero encountered his first "pagan" Indians and wrote:

> I gave praise to the Lord, kissing the ground, and thanking His Majesty for the fact that, after so many years of looking forward to it, He now permitted me to be among the pagans in their own country. . . . I saw something I could not believe when I had read of it, or had been told about it. It was this: they were entirely naked, as Adam in the garden, before sin. So they go, and so they presented themselves to us. . . . One after another, I put my hands on each of them, in sign of affection. I filled both their hands with dried figs, which they immediately began to eat. We received with show of much appreciation the presents they offered us, *viz*; a net of roasted *mescales* [cactuses], and four fish of more than medium size. . . . I was convinced that, before long, they would be caught in the apostolic and evangelical net.[48]

Three days out of Velicatá, Junípero wrote: "I had much trouble in standing on my feet, because the left one was much inflamed. . . . The swelling has reached halfway up my leg, which is covered with sores."[49] Governor Portolá tried to deter him from going further but Junípero replied:

> I trust that God will give me the strength to arrive at San Diego, as he has given me to arrive this far. If this should not be the case, I conform myself to His Most Holy Will. But even though I die on the road, I will not turn back. Although I would be buried here, I shall gladly remain among the pagans, if it be the will of God.[50]

As final alternative to being carried on a stretcher back to Loreto, Junípero asked the muleteer to prepare a poultice for his leg. He was hesitant, pleading that he was not a physician, but Junípero convinced him by saying: "Just imagine me to be an animal, [and] make me the same remedy you would apply to an animal."[51] The hot herb and tallow application worked, and by the next day he was walking and able to say Mass.

On 28 May, Junípero met more Indians who

> came with their nets [full] of cooked *mescal*, and all their weapons, which they laid on the ground. They started in to explain their use in battle, one after the other. They played all the parts both of the attacker and the attacked in such a vivid way, and with such address, that it was a pleasant moment of relaxation for us. . . . So far we had not seen any women among them, and, till now, I [Junípero] was anxious not to see them, because I feared that they went as naked as the men. But when, in the midst of all this entertainment, two women appeared, talking as rapidly and efficiently as that sex is accustomed to do, and when I saw them so decently covered that we would feel happy if no greater display of indecency was ever seen among the Christian women of the missions, I no longer

regretted their arrival. . . . [One] carried upon her head [a] present, the like of which I had never seen, a great pancake of a thing like dough, but full of thick fibers. I went to lay my hands upon her head, and she left the cake in my hands. She . . . immediately began to explain to me how it was eaten. The older woman spoke also, yelling louder than all the rest. . . . May God bless them.[52]

The terrain slowly improved as Junípero continued northward, and by 2 June he could write:

The thorns and rocks of [Lower] California have disappeared. . . . There are flowers in abundance and . . . when we came to our stopping place, we met the queen of flowers, the Rose of Castile [Wild Rose of California]. While I write this, I have in front of me a cutting from a rose-tree with three roses in full bloom, others opening out, and more than six unpetaled: Blessed be He who created them![53]

After passing through several Indian *rancherías* (villages), Junípero wrote about one:

[The Indians'] fine stature, deportment, conversation and gaiety won the hearts of all. They loaded us down with fish and abalones; they went out in their little canoes to fish especially for us; they put on their dances for our benefit. . . . All the gentiles have pleased me, but these in particular have won my heart.[54]

On 26 June, Junípero wrote:

[All the Indians] want my habit which they tug at by the sleeve. If I had given the habit to all who wanted it, there would be by this time a pretty large community of gentile friars. What I would like to imprint deep in their hearts is this: *Induimini Dominum Jesum Christum* [Put on the Lord Jesus Christ].[55]

Three days before arriving at San Diego, Junípero reflected on the journey:

We met with no hostile demonstrations, in fact just the reverse. On many occasions we were regaled by the gentiles, reversing the proverb: "The stingy man gives more than the naked man," because these naked Indians gave us more than many stingy men would have given us.[56]

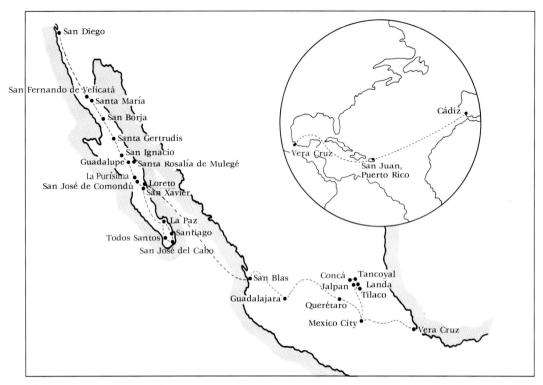

35. Serra's Mexican travels: 1749-1769.

36. Detail from an 1864 map of Mexico City, little changed from Serra's day. He first entered the city of 100,000 via Calzada de los Misterios (left arrow), a five-mile highway between Tepeyac (site of the Basilica of Our Lady of Guadalupe) and downtown, which was lined with fifteen monuments commemorating the mysteries of the Rosary. Just short of the cathedral, the viceroy's palace, and the archiepiscopal palace, all on the Plaza Mayor or "Zócalo," one of the largest public squares in the world, Serra turned right (middle). From there he walked up Avenida Tacuba-Hidalgo to San Fernando Church/Apostolic College (lower right), where he first arrived shortly after 9 a.m. on 1 January 1750.

37. San Fernando Church, sole remnant of the former Franciscan Apostolic College of San Fernando, which Serra was associated with from 1750 until his death. Named after Saint Ferdinand III, King of Castile (1198-1252, Spanish Third Order Franciscan), it was founded by royal decree on 15 October 1733. The cornerstone was laid on 19 October 1735, and the two-story, ten-cloistered church/*convento* complex was dedicated on 19 April 1755. San Fernando administered three mission fields between 1733 and 1853: Mexico's Sierra Gorda (1740-70); Lower California (1767-73); and Upper California, where 127 Fernandinos served between 1769 and 1853. Formally abolished in 1908, and the last of its buildings demolished in 1935, all that remains today of Serra's New World home-base is San Fernando Church. The four-domed, red *tezontle* (volcanic rock), and gray *cantería* (carved sandstone) Churrigueresque-style church (after José Churriguera, noted seventeenth-century Spanish architect who influenced Mexico's High Baroque period), is Mexico

City's second-largest after the cathedral. Saint Ferdinand defends the portal, in battle against the Moors. (Calle Guerrero and Avenida Tacuba-Hidalgo, Mexico City)

38. San Fernando interior circa 1800, when its original gold-leafed, richly-ornamented Churrigueresque altars were still intact. During the 1858-61 War of the Reform, much of Mexico's ecclesiastical property was destroyed, including San Fernando's interior and most of its furnishings.

39. San Fernando interior with replica *reredos*, installed in 1965. As in the original, Saint Ferdinand occupies the central niche above the Immaculate Conception. Serra said Mass here in 1750, during his years as a home missionary from 1758-67, and when he visited for the last time from California in 1773.

40. San Fernando transept and arched entrance to the former *convento*. The canvas dates from Serra's tenure and illustrates "The Glorification of the Name of Jesus" on the left, the Franciscan coat of arms and *Cinco Llagas* in the middle, and "The Franciscan Family Tree" on the right. In the screened-off seating area above, Serra practiced self-mortification "during the most silent part of the night." He "would betake himself to one of the tribunes of the choir. Although the place was so remote and the hour so quiet, there were friars who heard the cruel strokes. Nor were there lacking the curious who, desiring to learn the friar's identity, took the trouble to satisfy their curiosity, and they were edified."[57]

41. Iron and braided-wire *disciplina* traditionally believed to have been used by Serra in Upper California. 12" x 2-1/2." (Mission Carmel Museum, Carmel)

42. Mission Santiago de Jalpan Church, Jalpan, Querétaro, where Serra lived and worked from June 1750 to mid-September 1758. Located in the Sierra Gorda Mountains north of Mexico City, Jalpan was the capital of five missions founded among the Pame Indians by San Fernando College in 1744. The church, still in use today, is the spiritual and cultural heart of Jalpan (Nahuatl for "on top of the sandy hill"), population 2,000. It is the only complete, surviving building constructed by Serra, since all his Upper California missions were superseded by more permanent structures. Saint Peter and Saint Paul flank the scalloped *mezcla* (mortar) portal of the Churrigueresque façade. In the first level of niches between the columns, Saint Dominic is on the left and Saint Francis of Assisi on the right. Above the portal, the Franciscan coat of arms. In the second level of niches, Our Lady of Guadalupe, patroness of Mexico (left) and Our Lady of the Pillar, patroness of Spain (right). A clock has replaced Santiago (Saint James the Greater), patron of Spain, in the uppermost niche. (Plaza de Santiago, Jalpan)

43. Santiago de Jalpan interior with nineteenth-century Neoclassic *reredos*. Francisco Palóu described the original: "[The interior, 125 feet long by 35 feet wide, has a] corresponding transept and dome, and adjacent to it the sacristy (which was also vaulted); also a chapel dedicated to the Holy Sepulcher, which [Serra] adorned with statues and the Stations of Our Savior's Passion in order to draw the [Indians'] affections more closely to the devout ceremonies of Holy Week. The church was likewise adorned with *reredoses*, . . . and [six] side *reredoses*, all gilded."[58]

44. Title page from a novena booklet that Serra may have authored during his period as a San Fernando home missionary. The Spanish *Novena de Alabanzas en Honrra de la Puríssima Concepción de María SSma. con el Título de Prelada* (*Novena of Prayers in Honor of the Most Pure Conception of Holy Mary, Bearing the Title of Prelatess*) is a nine-day novena of prayers to the Virgin Mary. The booklet was first published by D. Xavier Sanchez, Mexico City, 1765, and a second-edition by Don Felipe de Zúñiga y Ontiveros in 1770. Fernandino authorship is anonymous except for title-page data that translates: "The faltering tongue of a humble subject of the seigniory of the Apostolic College of San Fernando offers it [the novena] to Mary's devoted." Prominent Mexican bibliographers have interpreted this as reference to Serra, most notably José Mariano Beristain y Souza in *Biblioteca Hispano Americana Septentrional* (*North American Hispanic Library*), Mexico City, 1796; and José Toribio Medina in *La Imprenta de México, 1539-1821* (*The Mexican Press, 1539-1821*), Mexico City, 1907. If Serra authored the *Novena*, then it is the only known publication of his writings during his lifetime. There is no evidence to indicate it was used in California during the mission period. 45 pages. 3" x 4." (Two complementary fragments form a whole: Manuscript 78, Junípero Serra Collection of Documents, Santa Barbara Mission Archive-Library, Santa Barbara; and Archdiocese of Los Angeles Archival Center, Mission Hills)

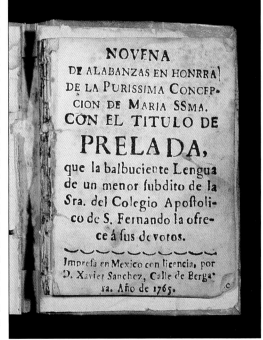

NOVENA
DE ALABANZAS EN HONRRA
DE LA PURISSIMA CONCEP-
CION DE MARIA SSMA.
CON EL TITULO DE
PRELADA,
que la balbuciente Lengua
de un menor subdito de la
Sra. del Colegio Apostoli-
co de S. Fernando la ofre-
ce á sus devotos.

Impresa en Mexico con licencia, por
D. Xavier Sanchez, Calle de Berga-
ra. Año de 1765.

45. Presidio-Mission Nuestra Señora de Loreto Church, Loreto, Lower California, where Serra lived and worked from April 1768 to April 1769. Named after the Virgin Mary under her appellation as Our Lady of Loreto, the *presidio-mission* was founded on 25 October 1697, as the capital and first in a chain of peninsular missions established by the Society of Jesus. When King Carlos II abruptly expelled the Jesuits from Spain and its possessions in June 1767, the fifteen missions and their furnishings were entrusted to the Franciscans of San Fernando college. The church, in a desert setting only a few hundred yards from the western shore of the Sea of Cortez, dominates the small town of Loreto with its new bell-tower (population 200 in Serra's day, 5,000 now). Our Lady of Loreto adorns the austere stone façade, and the Spanish inscription in the doorway's cornice bespeaks an illustrious past: "Head and Mother of the Missions of Lower and Upper California." (Calles Salvatierra and Misioneros, Loreto)

46. Mission Loreto interior with Neo-Churrigueresque *reredos* installed in 1956. Our Lady of Loreto in the central niche dates from the mission's founding. The cedar-beam ceiling is also original. From the sacristy of this church (through the arched doorway on the left in the sanctuary), Serra requisitioned the "Loreto silver" for the Upper California missions.

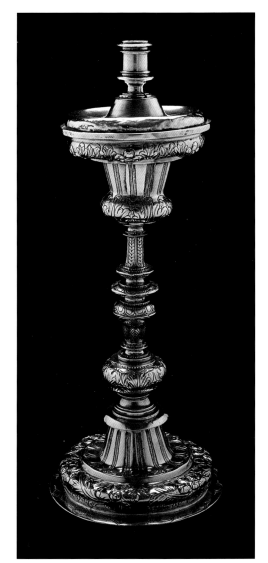

47. One of six matching Loreto silver altar candlesticks requisitioned by Serra from among "superfluous things which would not be missed by the old [Lower California] missions,"[59] and shipped to Upper California in 1769. Mission Loreto contributed "six large silver candlesticks two-thirds of a *vara* high [one Spanish *vara* equals 33 linear inches], a set of altar cards and a silver missal stand."[60] All nine pieces appear in Mission San Carlos Borromeo's 1770 *Inventario* (*Inventory*, a list of items donated by the Crown for a new mission), and were present at the 3 June 1770 founding. All are unmarked, which is consistent with their late-seventeenth-century manufacture date, since the *cedula real* (royal decree) requiring Mexican silver to bear the chief assayer's mark did not take effect until 1733. The candlesticks are assembled in sections from Mexican *repoussé* sheet silver (*repoussé* metalwork is chased on the outside and embossed on the inside to create a three-dimensional effect). Each has a cast cup and weighs 74 ounces Troy (including a wood core). 18" tall x 7-3/4" base diameter. (Mission Carmel Museum, Carmel)

48. Loreto silver altar card, one of two. The set originally consisted of three cards used by the priest during the recitation of the Mass. The *Lavábo* (I Will Wash) prayer, recited during the Offertory Rite washing of the hands, is pictured here. The cards, with chased lettering and *repoussé* borders, weigh 24 ounces Troy each (including a wood backing). The Latin translates: "With the pure in heart I Will wash my hands clean, and take my place among them at thy altar, Lord, listening there to the sound of thy praises, telling the story of all thy wonderful deeds. How well, Lord, I love thy house in its beauty, the place where thy own glory dwells! Lord, never count this soul for lost with the wicked, this life among the bloodthirsty: hands ever stained with guilt, palms ever itching for a bribe! Be it mine to guide my steps clear of wrong: deliver me in thy mercy. My feet are set on firm ground; where thy people gather, Lord, I will join in blessing thy name. Glory be to the Father, and to the Son, and to the Holy Spirit. As it was [in the beginning, is now, and ever shall be world without end. Amen]. To be added to the final Collect: And protect from all adversity our Pope, our Bishop, and our King, together with the royal offspring, the people, the army, who have been committed to your care; grant your peace in our time and drive all evil from your Church. Through Our Lord [Jesus Christ, your Son, Who lives and reigns with You in the unity of the Holy Spirit, God, forever and ever. Amen]. 12" x 10." (Mission Carmel Museum, Carmel)

49. Loreto silver missal stand with *repoussé*-decorated cross, Jesuit IHS emblem, and shell-leaf motif. Cast silver stand. 98 ounces Troy. 13" x 13" x 13" deep. (Mission Carmel Museum, Carmel)

50. Silver holy water stoup listed in Mission San Carlos Borromeo's 1770 founding *Inventario*, mentioned by Serra at the 3 June 1770 establishment of Monterey's *presidio*-mission when he "sprinkled with holy water all the fields," and used by Pope John Paul II during the Rite of Blessing before Mass at Monterey's Laguna Seca Raceway on 17 September 1987. Although the piece is not identified in any of the detailed Lower California requisition inventories, its decorative Jesuit iconography strongly links it to the former Jesuit missions of Lower California. It is the oldest item in Mission San Carlos Borromeo's silver collection, bearing the simplified Mexican royal hallmark required between 1579 and 1637. The stoup, used during the Asperges blessing ceremony, has *repoussé* strap-work design on the central section, bulbous base and spreading foot. A hollow, cast-silver handle detaches from two lion-head sockets and engraved figures depict Saint Ignatius Loyola with book and Jesuit emblem (rayed IHS monogram and three nails of the Crucifixion); Christ Child with globe; and the Annunciation. 88 ounces Troy. 10" tall x 11" bowl diameter. (Mission Carmel Museum, Carmel)

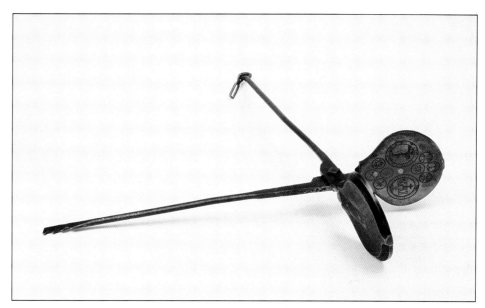

51. One of "four bake-iron[s] to make altar breads"[61] requisitioned by Serra from Lower California and shipped to Upper California in 1769. Engraved with various religious symbols including those of the Passion, the iron may have belonged to Mission Santa Clara. After the missions were secularized in the 1830s, it passed to the Castro-Moreno family of San Jose, where it remains today. 32" long x 7" diameter.

52. Ruins of Mission San Fernando de Velicatá, the first Indian mission founded by Serra. After its founding, the mission soon grew to include an *adobe* (sun-dried mud) church, *adobe* "mission house," storehouse, corral and crops irrigated by a small dam on the San Fernando River. From 1769 to 1773, 445 Baptisms, 167 weddings and 1 burial were performed. The Franciscans transferred the Lower California missions to the Dominican Order in 1773, and during their tenure (1773-1821), 2,572 Baptisms, 592 marriages and 2,156 burials were recorded. The mission was abandoned in 1821, for as an important supply link in the overland trail from Loreto to San Diego, it was exposed to the vicissitudes of epidemic, which slowly decimated the Indian population. Four twelve-foot *adobe* shafts, formerly a room in the mission quadrangle, are all that remain. (3 miles off Mexican Federal Highway 1, between El Rosario and Cataviña, Baja California Norte)

California: 1769-1784

On 1 July 1769, Junípero arrived "at the famous and wished for Port of San Diego, . . . on the bank of the port area, not far from its mouth, where the two [supply] packetboats were [already] at anchor."[62] In his words, "it was a day of much rejoicing and merriment for all,"[63] despite the fact that his left leg from the ankle up was "like the foot was before, one large wound."[64]

On 2 July, the "Feast of the Visitation of Our Lady," Junípero "sang a Mass of thanks to her Most Holy Spouse [Saint Joseph], patron of both expeditions of sea and land."[65] His first California Mass ("California" will hereinafter refer to the U.S. State of California) was celebrated at the site chosen for the new military *presidio* (from the Latin *praesidium*, garrison or fort) and Indian mission (a "school" of religion and civilization). Located two miles inland on a hill overlooking the bay near the San Diego River, and near the Cosoy Ranchería of the local Indians of the Kumeyaay ethnic and linguistic group, it was described by Junípero as

> [covered with] roses of Castile and trees in abundance . . . [and] so many vines
> grown by nature and without human help that it would mean little expense to
> follow the example of our good father Noah ["Noah, a man of the soil, was the
> first to plant a vineyard. When he drank some of the wine, he became drunk and
> lay naked inside his tent" [Genesis 20:21].[66]

On Sunday 16 July, Junípero and Governor Gaspar de Portolá established Presidio-Mission San Diego de Alcalá, California's first Christian settlement. Junípero sang a High Mass, preached a sermon, "raised the standard of the Holy Cross," and afterward "engaged in constructing primitive huts . . . [and] dedicat[ing one] as a temporary church."[67]

Calling San Diego's Indians the "west coast Indians," Junípero noted they were "much more gifted" than most. However, it was not easy to gain their trust. While attempting to perform his first California Baptism only a few weeks after his arrival, events did not unfold as planned. Just as he was about to pour the water,

> the pagans snatched the child and carried it away to their village. [Junípero's]
> grief at being frustrated in baptizing that child was so great that . . . he attributed
> it to his own sins. . . . When he would relate the incident, even many years later,
> he had to dry the tears running from his eyes.[68]

On 15 August, an Indian attack at San Diego endangered Junípero's life, about which he later wrote: "I held [a] picture . . . [of] Our Blessed and Spotless Queen . . . in one hand, and her Divine Crucified Son in the other when arrows were raining everywhere; and my thoughts were, that with such defense either I would not have to die, or that I would die well, great sinner that I am."[69] He was unharmed, although he did witness the death of a young Spaniard who had accompanied him from Lower California. He "absolve[d] him and help[ed] him to meet his end. . . . He expired on the ground before [Junípero], bathed in his own blood."[70]

At this early stage in California mission life, when conditions were still very primitive,

Junípero reflected on its prerequisites:

> Hardships they will . . . face, these men who come to sacrifice themselves in so holy an enterprise, as everyone knows. . . . Where distances are great, they are felt all the more keenly by one who is unwilling to be deprived of anything. However, I do not like to think that any of those who are coming are made of such poor clay. . . . [They] should be provided with a good stock of patience and charity, and their stay will be one of delight to them. It will enable them to amass riches, a wealth of sufferings. But what becomes of the ox that does not plough? And without plowing, can there be a harvest? . . . I put my trust in God that everything will turn out well.[71]

As 1769 progressed, scurvy killed many of the Spanish soldiers and sailors, provisions ran perilously low, and the first scheduled supply ship did not return from Mexico with replenishments. The dire situation forced a decision to abandon San Diego, and California, if the ship did not arrive soon. 20 March 1770 was chosen as "the limit," one day after the Solemnity of Saint Joseph.

"All these conversations and preparations were as so many arrows that pierced [Junípero's] fervent heart."[72] True to his motto *siempre adelante, nunca atrás*, he and fellow priest Juan Crespí decided to remain even if the settlement were abandoned, "relying on Almighty God's providence. . . . We are not dead yet, thank God. Having a little *tortilla* and the wild herbs of the field, what more do we want? . . . To a willing heart all is sweet."[73]

"Realizing how close was the feast of the most holy Patriarch Saint Joseph," Junípero proposed that a nine-day novena to Saint Joseph

> be started. This was agreed upon, and all the men attended. The novena prayers were held after the daily recitation of the Rosary. Saint Joseph's day arrived, and the feast of this great saint was celebrated with a High Mass and sermon. Everything belonging to the expeditionary force had already been prepared for departure. . . . But on that very afternoon [at 3 p.m.] God willed to satisfy the ardent longings of His servant [Junípero] through the intercession of Saint Joseph, and to bring comfort to all by allowing them to see clearly and distinctly a ship [on the southern horizon]. The men attributed it to a miracle, through the intercession of the holy Patriarch that on his very feast day, the day the expedition had set as its term of stay, the ship was descried.[74]

Junípero's heart was filled with "singular joy and happiness" and he

> ceaselessly thanked God, as well as the blessed Saint, consoler of the afflicted, Saint Joseph, whom he openly acknowledged as the bestower of so special a favor. Showing his gratitude to the Saint, he sang a High Mass in his honor with the greatest solemnity. . . . This holy devotion he continued [on the nineteenth of each month] up to the very last month of his life.[75]

With replenished supplies and a restored sense of purpose, the expedition decided not to abandon San Diego. They continued north to Monterey for a second time (Governor Portolá had led an unsuccessful land expedition from San Diego to Monterey in autumn 1769, but failed to recognize Monterey's unassuming harbor as described within crescent-shaped Monterey Bay by previous Spanish explorer Sebastián Vizcaíno). Junípero entered the bay aboard the *San Antonio* on 31 May 1770, and first stepped ashore at Monterey on 1 June.

On Pentecost Sunday 3 June, at a "little *enramada* chapel and altar . . . erected in that little valley, and under the same live-oak, close to the beach"[76] where Vizcaíno and his Carmelite chaplains had said Mass more than 167 years before on 17 December 1602, Junípero and Governor Portolá established Presidio-Mission San Carlos Borromeo, California's second. In Junípero's words:

> Our arrival was greeted by the joyful sound of the bells suspended from the branches of the oak tree. Everything being in readiness, and having put on alb and stole, and kneeling down with all the men before the altar, I intoned the hymn *Veni, Creator Spiritus* [Come, Holy Spirit] at the conclusion of which, after invoking the help of the Holy Spirit on everything we were about to perform, I blessed the salt and water. Then we all made our way to a gigantic cross which was all in readiness and lying on the ground. With everyone lending a hand we set it in an upright position. I sang the prayers for its blessing. We set it in the ground and then, with all the tenderness of our hearts, we venerated it. I sprinkled with holy water all the fields around. And thus, after raising aloft the standard of the King of Heaven, we unfurled the flag of Our Catholic Monarch likewise. As we raised each one of them, we shouted at the top of our voices: "Long live the Faith! Long live the King!" All the time the bells were ringing, and our rifles were being fired, and from the boat came the thunder of the big guns. . . . I began the High Mass, [and] a sermon after the Gospel; and, as long as the Mass lasted, it was accompanied with many salvos of cannon. . . . As a conclusion to the liturgical celebration, standing up I intoned the *Te Deum Laudámus* [We Praise Thee, O God]; we sang it slowly, and solemnly, right to the end. . . . While I was making my thanksgiving after the Mass of the day, the officers proceeded to the act of formal possession of that country in the name of His Catholic Majesty, unfurling and waving once more the royal flag, pulling grass, moving stones and other formalities according to law, all accompanied with cheers, ringing of bells, cannonades, etc. In addition, there was a banquet served afterwards to all of us gathered together on the beach; later a walk at sunset along the ocean concluded the celebration.[77]

The new *presidio*-mission was built on a "pretty plain about a rifle shot from the beach."[78] In describing his new home where he lived from 4 June 1770 to 24 August 1771, Junípero wrote to his nephew in Majorca: "Just get out a map of America and look at it. . . . Follow the [west] coast to the north, . . . you will find on some maps the name: Port of Monterey. Well, it is there . . . that your uncle is living."[79]

To provide a less confining environment for the Indians away from the soldiers, Junípero decided to sever the mission from the *presidio*. In August 1771, he selected a site about five miles south of Monterey on "the banks of the Carmel River and in view of the sea, . . . a truly delightful spot, which, thanks to its plentiful supply both of land and water, gives promise of abundant harvests."[80] On 24 August, a "large cross [was] raised and [fixed] in the center of the area selected for the mission."[81] Junípero blessed it and said Mass under an *enramada*, Mission San Carlos Borromeo del Río Carmelo's (Mission Carmel's) first temporary church. This mission would be his home and administrative headquarters for the remaining fourteen years of his life, as well as his burial site.

Completed for Christmas Eve Mass 1771, Mission Carmel's second church, built on approximately the same site as the first, consisted of

> one . . . whitewashed . . . cell . . . in the principal building . . . divided into six rooms, all with their doors and locks. . . . The walls are made of stout limbs and pine trees, stripped off and well trimmed, the spaces in between filled with stones, rubble or branches and stuccoed all over both inside and out. The roof is made of thick beams of both pine and cypress well trimmed, and covered with poles and straw protected by plastered clay and mud. . . . Some of [the] doors are made of a red wood whose name we do not know, but which is from a fine and noble tree [California Coast Redwood].[82]

Known as a *jacal*, this building also served as Junípero's first home and mission headquarters. He wrote:

> The said house is furnished with water jars, a bookcase, scissor-shaped seats, some covered with woven reeds, others with leather; two large benches, one larger than the other, two tables, cupboards, etc. In short, we have a place to live in, and can put under lock and key what is sent to us. . . . But because it is not firmly nailed together, we did not possess any nails, an entrance can easily be effected by knocking down or pushing aside some of the poles. . . . May God look to it![83]

Along with its simple structures, the mission began operation with "nine full grown cows, and a bull for breeding, two heifers, six little calves"[84] and a "miserable garden."

Three more missions were founded within the next year: San Antonio de Padua on 14 July 1771; San Gabriel Arcángel on 8 September 1771; and San Luís Obispo on 1 September 1772. After Junípero's first complete tour of the fledgling five-mission chain in autumn 1772, he did not like what he saw. Provisions were irregular, Indian-military relations were steadily deteriorating, and many changes needed to be made. With "no human recourse" the *presidente* turned to "God as the Lord of this vineyard, asking . . . assistance of Him in the holy sacrifice of the Mass and prayer . . . for light to know what would be most pleasing to Him."[85]

The nearly sixty-year old Junípero decided to travel to Mexico City to personally appeal to the new viceroy for an improvement in mission conditions. After a fifteen-day voyage from San Diego to the Mexican west-coast port of San Blas, he spent the next three months making his way east across the countryside to Mexico City. Presaging the future he wrote: "If only [I] could go there and fly back immediately."[86] Traveling companion Juan Evangelista, a Mission

Carmel Indian boy, was stricken with severe fever en route and Junípero, twice "at the gates of death," later wrote:

> This trip to Mexico has broken me down considerably, since because of the fatigue of the journey, I arrived in the city of Guadalajara [at the Convento de San Francisco, 360 miles northwest of Mexico City] burning with fever. A few days later I was advised to receive the Last Sacraments, and was in real danger. Later on the constant fever turned into an intermittent one, and I continued my trip in that condition. On arriving at Querétaro [at the Convento de Santa Cruz, 130 miles northwest of Mexico City] I again was so ill, that they, too, advised me to receive the Last Sacraments. But in a short time I recovered, and finally I arrived. . . . It was some time before I recovered my strength, and I suffered much from loss of appetite.[87]

While at San Fernando College from February to September 1773, Junípero was described as

> a lion, giving in only to fever, for none of the ailments that constantly afflict him, especially shortness of breath, chest pains, and sores on his legs and feet, have ever kept him from his apostolic duties. . . . Often he has seemed dead and suddenly brought back to life . . . by the sole virtue of Divine Providence. For the austerity of his life, his humility, charity and other virtues, he is truly worthy of being counted among the imitators of the Apostles.[88]

After a brief period of recuperation, Junípero conferred with New Spain's Viceroy Antonio María Bucareli y Ursúa ("vice-king" of Mexico for Carlos III of Spain), and was ordered to present his requests in writing for formal presentation at court. He drafted a thirty-two point *Representación* (*Petition*), which succinctly outlined California's needs and problems. The viceroy was so impressed with Junípero and his presentation that he

> constituted himself judge, attorney and patron of the cause. He summoned a meeting of the Junta de Guerra y Real Hacienda [Council of War and Royal Ministry of Finance], over which His Excellency himself presided. After the members had read and discussed the document point by point, all voted in favor of the [spiritual] conquest. They even granted more than [Junípero] requested.[89]

The outcome of Junípero's *Representación* was a "Bill of Rights" for California, the first piece of legislation aimed specifically at the province. Codified into law via a new *Reglamento* (*Regulation*, a civil constitution) which took effect on 1 January 1774, it provided for expansion of the mission system, placement of Indian welfare exclusively under missionary control to prevent most military abuses, redefined *presidio*-mission relations, increased the supply and distribution of food, animals, supplies and mail, and encouraged Mexican emigration from Mexico to California. A 1779 *Reglamento*, drafted to remedy defects in the 1774 document, remained intact as California's fundamental civil code until Spain ceded to Mexico in 1821.

With his business settled, Junípero prepared to leave Mexico City. He discouraged talk of being elected San Fernando College administrator, may have sat for a portrait, and repeated the same act of humility performed when leaving Palma twenty-four years prior. "Touch[ing] the hearts of all in such a way that they shed copious tears,"[90] he knelt and kissed the feet of each member of the community, knowing he would never see them again. Sometime in mid-September he departed for "that far distant [California] vineyard of the Lord," and added: "[California] is the place for me to live in and, I hope to God, that is where I shall die, [although] seeing that at present the state of my health is none too good, I will have to make the trip somewhat slowly."[91]

After almost two year's absence, and a return journey from San Diego to Monterey by land, Junípero and Juan Evangelista finally reached Mission Carmel on 11 May 1774. Monterey-Carmel's worst supply shortage, caused by shipment irregularities, had been alleviated by a full store of supplies from the *Santiago*, which arrived in Monterey a few days before Junípero. Having subsisted on peas, herbs, milk and offerings from the Indians, the community now celebrated as ham, jerked beef, corn, beans, chickpeas, lentils, rice, flour, peppers, olive oil, lard, wine, brandy, brown sugar and chocolate were dispensed.

Mission Carmel's conditions began to improve and priest and Indian alike "appl[ied] themselves in earnest to work, some with hoe in hand, some with mold making *adobe*, others in reaping and harvesting the wheat, in housing it in the barns and in [many] other occupation[s]."[92] The mission compound had been expanded during Junípero's absence and now consisted of a larger, new *jacalón* church of logs/planks, thirty *varas* in length, "rather spacious and well made, . . . [and] somewhat adorned with paintings"[93] (this was Mission Carmel's third mission church, first used on Christmas Day 1773). Also of the same construction, a new office, guardhouse, surgeon house, two servant houses, blacksmith/carpenter shop and quarters, granary and an *adobe* oven. Junípero described the mission's 1774 garden as "splendid, full of vegetables,"[94] due to a new irrigation system that drew water from the Carmel River. He summed up this turning point in prosperity when he wrote that "Monterey and its missions" should no longer be looked upon "as the China or Ceuta [a Spanish North African city known for its prison] of exile."[95]

Junípero learned that total Mission Carmel Baptisms had only risen from fifteen to seventy-four during his absence. He now "cast the net among the pagans," inviting them to join the mission's 400 resident Indians. Seventy-two Baptisms were performed within the next two months, as described by Junípero

> on children not over eight years old. . . . To hear them pray, and answer questions, well versed in all the questions and answers of Christian Doctrine; to hear them sing, to see them all dressed in worsted clothes and woolens; to see how happy they are at play, and how they run up to the Father, as if they had known him all their lives; all of this gladdens the heart, and impels one gratefully to give praise to God.[96]

On 5 November 1775, Mission San Diego was attacked and burned by nearly 1,000 local Tipai and Ipai Indians, upset by continued abuses from *presidio* soldiers. When Junípero learned that resident missionary Father Luís Jayme and two tradesmen had been killed, he wrote: "I would welcome such a fate, with God's grace and favor. . . . Thanks be to God, now indeed the land has been watered [with martyred blood]; certainly now the conversion of the San Diego

Indians will be achieved."[97] He wrote to Viceroy Bucareli, asking for

> a formal statement drawn up by Your Excellency . . . in so far as it concerns me, and the other religious who at present are subject to me, or will be in the future, . . . [that] if ever the Indians, whether they be gentile or Christian, killed [us], they should be forgiven.[98]

His request was granted, and he went to San Diego the following year to help rebuild the mission. Carlos, alleged leader of the attack, was a baptized Indian of the Cuimac Ranchería, and he eventually returned to the mission seeking asylum. Junípero once again appealed to Viceroy Bucareli and successfully obtained amnesty and rehabilitation for Carlos and fellow conspirators. He wrote:

> Great was our joy when we secured a general amnesty. . . . They are now all living in the said mission; they are held in high esteem, and receive every attention from the religious there. . . . Because of our love of God, we set them free, so that they might lead better lives.[99]

Around the same time a rumor spread that well-armed Salinas Valley Sanjone Indians were on their way to attack Mission Carmel. Envisioning martyrdom at the hands of "gentiles," Junípero was "full of joy . . . the hour has arrived; . . . there is thus nothing else to do but to be courageous and prepare ourselves for whatever God shall decree."[100] Carmel's other priests received no sleep that night because Junípero's "abounding joy did not allow him to stop talking. He recounted many similar situations in order to give [them] courage,"[101] but the attack never materialized.

Junípero continued to oversee the establishment of new missions: San Francisco de Asís (9 October 1776); San Juan Capistrano (1 November 1776); Santa Clara de Asís (12 January 1777); and San Buenaventura (31 March 1782). He never complained of illness, lack of food or even "tunics falling to pieces," but when it came to the "harvesting of souls" or matters concerning his "tender [mission] plants," he was zealously concerned and "always on fire with a longing to see the spiritual conquests in which we are engaged, show signs of progress."[102] In using "all possible measures" to establish more missions,

> there were not lacking persons of good standing and character who, knowing the effectiveness of Father Junípero in projecting new missions, said of him: "Father Junípero is indeed a saintly man; but in this matter of seeking to build missions, he is an annoying saint."[103]

When journeying north or south from Mission Carmel, Junípero traveled along El Camino Real (The "Royal" or "King's Highway"), the land artery that linked travel and supply routes within Spain's New World empire. The missions were eventually separated by roughly one day's journey along its El Camino, although in Junípero's day there were not as many "steppingstones." As he wrote, they were spaced "so that every third day one might sleep in a village . . . and passage through all the country [was] made easy."[104] Contrary to legend, he did not walk from

California mission to mission, except once in 1779, from Mission Carmel to Mission Santa Clara (a distance of about 80 miles in two days). He normally rode a mule, occasionally a horse, and was accompanied by a military guard. As a contemporary stated: "California is two hundred and five leagues in length. It is impossible to traverse the distance on foot. The distances from one mission to another are immense."[105]

Travel could be dangerous, as in November 1776 when Junípero was threatened by a large group of Indians near San Juan Capistrano, "all painted and well-armed, emitting fearful yells, their arrows aimed in readiness;"[106] or poignant, as in December of the same year when rough seas blocked passage through a section of the Santa Barbara Channel. Local Indians carried Junípero up the steep trail and along the cliffs, and he later wrote:

> Tears welled up into my eyes when I saw with what good will they came to my assistance. . . . Walking along the road with me, [they would] break out into song each time I started a tune for them. . . and would come up for me to make the sign of the Cross on their foreheads. . . . All are as friendly as can be . . . young and old crying out: "*Amar a Dios, Padre Viejo! Viva Jesús!*" [Love God, Old Father! Hail Jesus!]. And if they tell the truth, that I am old, what am I to do?[107]

Junípero tended to spiritual matters when visiting missions, and concentrated on administering Confirmation after being granted a ten-year faculty. Since he was not a bishop, permission was needed from the Vatican, and the patent, signed by Pope Clement XIV, took effect on 16 July 1774. However, a series of bureaucratic technicalities in Mexico and California prevented Junípero's receiving the original patent until 20 June 1778. On Monday 29 June, he confirmed for the first time, administering the Sacrament to ninety young Indians at Mission Carmel.

Bureaucratic difficulties also hampered Junípero's relations with civil authorities, most notably Governor Felipe de Neve, who resided at Monterey. He was capable but aloof, and often antagonized the missionaries. After one particularly tense encounter concerning the proposed election of Indian *alcaldes* (mayors) at each mission, which the missionaries opposed because the office was often abused "to indulge in numerous crimes," Junípero wrote:

> During the rest of the day I felt wretched, being quite incapable of throwing off the obsession, and arguing with myself in a thousand ways, as to what I should do. I started a letter to the said *Señor*, . . . yet, with every sentence I wrote, something came up against it. . . . I went over the matter again and again in my mind. . . . [Eventually] the night was far spent, and [if] I did not lie down for a while, even though I did not feel sleepy, I would be useless [the next day]. So I made up my mind to lie down, fully dressed as I was. I got to the alcove, with the idea of finding some rest in sensible reflections and in fixing my mind on some religious subject. But it was all to no purpose. I just had to break out with: "What is the meaning of it all, O Lord?" And a voice within me seemed to reply in very clear words: "*Prudentes sicut serpentes, et simplices sicut columbae*" [Be clever as snakes and innocent as doves, Matthew 10:16]. And I felt a new man again: "Yes, Lord, yes, Lord," I said, "thus it will be with your grace." I fell off to sleep.

At the usual time I arose to say my Office [of prayers]. . . . And so the program I have outlined is this: whatever the gentleman wishes to be done should be done, but in such wise that it should not cause the least change among the Indians or disturb the routine.[108]

Governor Neve's plan was implemented, but eventually abandoned after meeting with little cooperation from Indian and missionary alike.

In Mission Carmel's 1779 *Informe* (a statistical annual *Report* required by the Crown), Junípero mentioned Mission Carmel's Jacalón Grande Church. This fourth church superseded the previous one at the end of 1778. With an *adobe* façade, a sacristy and a whitewashed, painted interior, it was the largest of Carmel's *jacalones*, "serv[ing] with all possible dignity . . . and it [was] large enough for the whole *pueblo* [town]."[109] Also, conversion to an all-*adobe* compound began and the mission was now agriculturally self-sufficient, with "farmers, birdcatchers, field-clearers, grain-cleaners and every other kind of farm workers coming and going about their business."[110] The Indians had enough

> *pozole* [meat and vegetable stew] and *atole* [wheat or cornmeal gruel] cost what it may. . . . When we run very short, some permissions [for the Indians to feed themselves in the wild] are given or we make the [food] a little thinner. We manage as best as we can, and the population is fat and well-satisfied.[111]

As 1781 drew to a close, Junípero's Majorcan friend and co-missionary at Carmel, Juan Crespí, became very ill. With no physician at Monterey, Junípero consulted his *Florilegium* (Medical Anthology), hoping to ease his "fatigue . . . chest trouble . . . and the swelling of his feet."[112] To no avail, he died of congestive heart failure at age 50 on 1 January 1782, and Junípero buried him the next day in the sanctuary of the church near the main altar. He penned his obituary in the mission's *Libro de Difuntos* (*Book of Deaths*), wherein he described Juan as a "companion of many years. . . [and] a true religious."[113]

Upon returning from his last Confirmation tour of Southern California in December 1783, Junípero was welcomed by the sight of a newly-completed, all-*adobe* church in "this the happiest year of the mission."[114] The completed fifth Mission Carmel church, the "Serra Adobe Church," measuring "forty by eight *varas* with a thatched roof,"[115] contained three sandstone burial vaults in the sanctuary (Juan Crespí was reinterred in the left vault, Junípero buried in the central vault in 1784, and Fermín de Lasuén in the right one in 1803), and was large enough for all the Indians to pray in "twice daily with the priest."

Mission Carmel's resident Indian population reached 645 in 1783, and agricultural productivity continued to increase. Livestock consisted of 500 cattle "large and small," 220 sheep and goats, 25 pigs, 8 "riding and draft mules," 20 "tame and broken horses," 90 "mares with their colts, also with them, two young mules from the time we had a jack" and 1 "old ass that may be with foal."[116]

On 17 April 1784, Junípero wrote a congratulatory letter to fellow-missionary Fermín de Lasuén at Mission San Diego after his mission became the first to administer 1,000 Baptisms. He wrote:

I had a notion, a piece of excusable, self-complacency, that I would be the first among the four who were close to the mark [Missions Carmel, San Diego, San Gabriel and San Antonio], to reach that milestone. But hail to San Diego! Here we are still eight short of reaching a thousand. But I am consoling myself with the thought that by [the end of] April we will reach the mark that San Diego reached in March. But, in either case, may the glory and honor be God's alone![117]

When Junípero performed Mission Carmel's 1,000th Baptism on 3 June 1784, he gave the Indian adult male the Christian name Millan Deogracias. Millan (after Saint Emillian Cucullatus) is very close to *millar*, Spanish for "one thousand." When combined with *Deogracias*, the play on words creates, "A thousand, thank God."

Slowing considerably by mid-1784, Junípero sensed himself "breaking up in health" and prepared to die. On 26 May, he completed his last trip, a Confirmation tour of the northern missions. At Carmel, he celebrated the Sacraments for the last time: on 14 June, his last marriage, that of Conrado José and Carola María, both local Christian Indians; on 6 July, his last Confirmation to Mustíola María, age ten; on 30 July, his last funeral, for Roque Juan Cordero, an Indian and "father of various Christians." Before Roque died, Junípero heard his Confession and administered Viaticum/Anointing of the Sick. On 2 August, the feast of Saint Pope Stephen I, he administered his last Baptism to an eight-day old Indian girl and named her Estefana Francisca. The date he offered his last Mass is unknown.

On 8 August, after having spent "half [his] life . . . at a writing desk,"[118] Junípero penned his last letter. Written to San Fernando College Guardian Juan Sancho, it closed with: "What I appreciate most of all are the prayers to Our Immaculate Queen so that here we may achieve success and afterwards Heaven. . . . Your affectionate and devoted subject, Fray Junípero Serra."[119]

Francisco Palóu, called from Mission San Francisco, optimistically assessed Junípero's health after hearing his strong singing voice on 18 August. Replied a soldier who had known him since 1769: "There is no basis for hope: he is ill. This saintly priest is always well when it comes to praying and singing, but he is nearly finished."[120] The following day, Junípero was to sing his monthly High Mass in honor of Saint Joseph. He was too weak however, so Francisco acted as substitute and Junípero sang with the Indian choir.

On 22 August, Monterey's royal surgeon came to assist Junípero and applied hot poultices to his chest. However, the pain, congestion and phlegm persisted, and nothing could be done for his "old lung trouble." Contemporary historians and physicians have suggested asthma or tuberculosis as source of his prolonged illness and eventual cause of death. However, his age, strenuous lifestyle, chest ailment and ulcerated leg certainly add up to Francisco's simple diagnosis of a "worn-out body."[121]

On 24 August, Junípero was still working, "cut[ting] up and distribut[ing] cloth to the neophytes to cover their nakedness."[122] He gave half of the blanket that covered his bed of planks to the "old chicken woman," an Indian so nicknamed in 1773 for having made a meal of the nascent mission's only hen and its chicks.

On 26 August, Junípero arose much weaker, having spent a bad night. He made his Last Confession to Francisco "amid many tears, and with a clear mind just as if he were well."[123]

On 27 August, Junípero awakened at dawn and requested Viaticum. Rather than having

49

the Last Eucharist brought to him, he eschewed tradition, stating that he "wanted to receive Him in church, since if he could walk there, there was no need for the Lord to come to him."[124] Having traveled 23,000 miles during his career, Junípero now walked his last few hundred yards to the sanctuary of the church, where he knelt and began to sing

> *Tantum ergo, Sacramentum, veneremur cernui* [Down in adoration falling, Lo, the Sacred Host we hail], . . . with tears in his eyes, . . . and with the sonorous voice he always used, as if nothing were the matter, affecting us all so deeply that we could not follow him in the singing. I [Francisco] administered the holy Viaticum . . . and when the service was finished he remained in the same posture on his knees, thanking the Lord.[125]

A large contingent of soldiers and Indians escorted Junípero back to his cell and "some shed tears from devotion and tenderness, others out of sadness and sorrow because they would be left without their beloved *padre*."[126] He passed the rest of the day in silence, drinking only a bit of broth for dinner. He felt worse that evening and Francisco administered the Last Sacraments. He did not sleep well, and occasionally sat on the floor supported by Indians who had come to visit, or kneeling next to his bed.

Appearing more at ease with the new dawn on Saturday 28 August, Junípero welcomed the officers and royal chaplain from a visiting ship. He thanked them for coming and asked them for a "favor and work of mercy; throw a bit of earth upon my body, and I shall be greatly indebted to you."[127] To Francisco he said: "I desire you to bury me in the church, quite close to Father Fray Juan Crespí for the present; and when the stone church is built, they may put me wherever they want."[128] He promised that "if the Lord in his infinite mercy grants me that eternal happiness, which I do not deserve because of my faults, . . . I shall pray for all [dwellers in these missions] and for the conversion of so many pagans whom I leave unconverted."[129]

Francisco sprinkled his cell with holy water around noon, and a little while later Junípero fell to his knees and said: "Great fear has come upon me; I have a great fear. Read me the Commendation for a Departing Soul, and say it aloud so I can hear it."[130] The long series of prayers, beginning with: "Depart, O Christian soul, out of this sinful world, in the name of God, the Father Almighty," brought a calming smile to Junípero's face as he attentively responded with the proper "Amens."

The visitors left the room and Junípero prayed alone until one o'clock. Francisco then brought him a cup of broth and Junípero whispered, undoubtedly in their native Mallorquín: "*Idò anem ara a descansar*" (Now, let us go to rest).[131] It was *siesta* time and he had not slept for over thirty hours. Removing his mantle, he laid down on the rough bed of boards covered with a half-blanket, put his head on the pillow and clasped his crucifix against his breast, the same one he had carried since leaving Majorca (now lost).

After leaving Junípero alone for a short time, Francisco returned and

> found him just as we had left him a little before, but now asleep in the Lord, without having given any sign or trace of agony, his body showing no other sign of death than the cessation of breathing; on the contrary, he seemed to be sleeping. We piously believe that he went to sleep in the Lord a little before two

in the afternoon, on the feast of Saint Augustine, . . . and that he went to receive in Heaven the reward of his apostolic labors.[132]

So ended Junípero's life at age 70 years, 9 months and 4 days. He had been a Franciscan for almost 54 years, a priest for 45 and an apostolic missionary for 35. In California alone he had baptized over 6,000 Indians and confirmed 5,308.

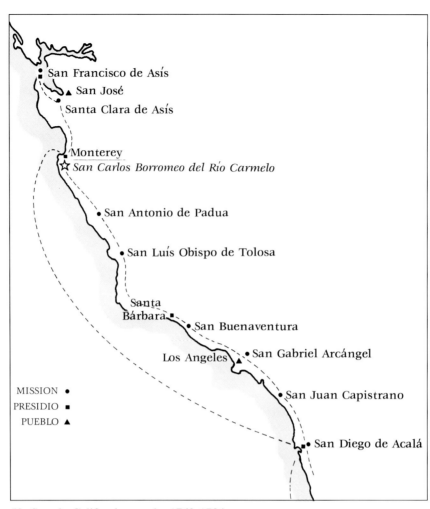

MISSION ●
PRESIDIO ■
PUEBLO ▲

53. Serra's California travels: 1769-1784.

54. San Diego Bay's "Spanish Landing," where the four contingents of the Portolá-Serra Expedition first reunited after their land and sea journeys from Lower California. On 11 April 1769, the supply ship *San Antonio* completed its voyage from La Paz, Lower California to San Diego Bay, followed by the *San Carlos* on 29 April. A third ship, the *San José*, was lost at sea and never found. The first land party, led by Captain Fernando de Rivera y Moncada, arrived on 14 May. On 1 July, Serra and Governor Portolá arrived and their reunion took place somewhere along the east bank of the bay's mud flats (arrow), little changed from their day in this 1937 photograph before the flats were dredged.

55. "Spanish Landing" today, reconfigured and converted into Spanish Landing Park. (North Harbor Drive, San Diego)

56. Typical plan of a California mission at its founding with *enramada*, cross and bells. This circa 1900 photograph commemorates the site of Mission San Diego's former *asistencia* (assistant or "satellite" mission). Located sixty miles east of San Diego, "Mission Santa Ysabel" was founded in 1818. The two bells, inscribed "*N.S. de Loreto 1729*" and "*San Pedro 1767*," were Mission San Diego's original bells, having been shipped from Lower California in 1769. They were stolen in 1930 and have never been found.

57. Presidio Hill, San Diego, circa 1895, where Presidio-Mission San Diego de Alcalá was founded on 16 July 1769 and where Serra lived from 1 July 1769 to 15 April 1770. After Mission San Diego was moved six miles inland in 1774 (into the valley on the left of the photograph), Presidio Hill remained just that, a *presidio* military fortification. An enclosed stockade, bounded roughly by the fenced area on the slope, served as the only source of military protection between San Diego and Santa Barbara. The *presidio* began to fall into ruin during the Mexican period (1821-46), and after American annexation (1848) the abandoned site was used for grazing cattle. This "cradle of California civilization" was also starting point of its historic El Camino Real and site of the future state's first Christian cemetery. Somewhere near the two palm trees lie the unmarked

graves of nearly sixty soldiers and sailors who died of scurvy during the 1769 Portolá-Serra Expedition. Serra helped bury them, his first burials within the state. The two palms, known as the "Serra Palms," may have been planted during the Spanish period. The tallest one fell during a storm in the early-twentieth century and the second was removed in 1957 due to "pink palm fungus, age and the effects of a quantity of bullets . . . [which] pitted the lower trunk and were believed to have been fired into it before the turn of the century by U.S. soldiers from the Presidio."[133]

58. Presidio Hill today. Atop it sits the Junípero Serra Museum dedicated in 1929, and a cross faced with floor tiles excavated from the original *presidio*. Commissioned by the "Order of Panama" civic club, the cross was blessed and dedicated on 27 September 1913. It commemorates the approximate site of the first cross raised by Serra in California, his first celebration of Mass within the state, and his first California mission. The mounds of earth on the lower right are unexcavated portions of the south wing of the *presidio*, and the grassy area is part of its inner *plaza*. (Presidio Drive, San Diego)

59. Mission San Diego Basilica. Serra did not live to see the present church, completed in 1813. In August 1774, the mission was moved six miles inland from the original Presidio Hill location to this site. This was done for agricultural purposes and to distance the Indians from the *presidio* soldiers, considered a bad influence. Serra visited the mission a total of six times (including the founding), the first three at the original site and the last three at the present one. (10818 San Diego Mission Road, San Diego)

60. Mission San Diego's original copper baptismal font, requisitioned by Serra from Mission San Luís Gonzaga, Lower California, and shipped to California in 1769. The handwrought font is mentioned in Mission San Diego's 1770 *Inventario*: "A copper baptismal font with its latch."[134] It survived the Indian attack and burning of the mission in 1775, and was kept there until 1834 when the mission was abandoned, after which it was eventually moved to the Chapel of the Immaculate Conception in San Diego's "Old Town," and then to Mission San Luís Rey. 8" tall x 16" diameter. (Mission San Luís Rey Museum, Oceanside)

61. *San Diego de Alcalá*, namesake of Mission San Diego. The name was first applied to the bay by Sebastián Vizcaíno, who entered it on 10 November 1602, two days short of Saint Didacus' feast day. When the Portolá-Serra Expedition settled the region, they reaffirmed the name. Serra mentioned the painting on 2 July 1770 when he unexpectedly found it, along with rolled-up canvases of Saint Charles Borromeo and Saint Bonaventure, aboard the *San Antonio* supply ship in Monterey. "His delight knew no bounds,"[135] and he blessed the anonymously donated works, and displayed *San Diego* for a short time at Mission San Carlos Borromeo. He then "sent [it] to the mission dedicated to that saint,"[136] since each mission was customarily provided with a patron saint painting at its founding. The painting survived the Indian burning of Mission San Diego, albeit "wrinkled for having suffered the sacrilegious mistreatment by the Indians."[137] Displayed at San Diego's Royal Presidio Chapel for a time after 1783, it was eventually moved to San Diego's Chapel of the Immaculate Conception and then to Mission San Luís Rey. After a 1987 restoration it was returned to Mission San Diego. The unsigned oil on canvas is attributed to José de Paez (1715-1790, prolific Mexican "Artist to the California Missions"). Saint Didacus of Alcalá (1400-1463, Spanish Franciscan brother) wears a brown Franciscan habit, halo and stands on a cloud assisted by angels. He holds a cross and basket of flowers in reference to the legend of his miraculous ability to change flowers into bread for the poor. 30" x 37-1/2." (Mission San Diego Basilica, San Diego)

62. *Monterey: Father Serra's Landing Place*, a fanciful oil on canvas depiction of Monterey's 3 June 1770 founding, painted by Leon Trousset in 1877.

63. Monterey's Vizcaíno-Serra landing cove. This 1878 view shows the cove (left arrow) before it was filled in; the Vizcaíno-Serra oak tree and commemorative cross in the ravine (right); and the Royal Presidio Chapel, now known as San Carlos Cathedral (middle), site of Monterey's *presidio*, and the mission before Serra moved it to Carmel.

64. "California's Plymouth Rock," the Vizcaíno-Serra *quercus agrifolia* (coast live oak) in full growth in Monterey's Vizcaíno-Serra landing cove, circa 1880. Under the shade of this tree with branches so close to the shore of Monterey Harbor that they "bath[ed] in the waters of the sea at high tide,"[138] Sebastián Vizcaíno and his Carmelite chaplains offered Mass on 17 December 1602. As the first recorded Europeans to step ashore at Monterey (named by Vizcaíno for New Spain's incumbent viceroy, Gaspar de Zúñiga Acevedo y Fonseca, Condé de Monterrey), this event predates the landing of the Pilgrims at Plymouth Rock (1620). On 3 June 1770, Serra and Governor Portolá used the same landmark oak described by Vizcaíno to confirm their "re-discovery" of Monterey Bay, and under its branches enacted the founding of Presidio-Mission San Carlos Borromeo for Spain. The landing site figured prominently during the remainder of the mission period, since it was near the loading and disembarkation point, and later the Custom House. The tree continued to grow despite sustaining severe lightning damage sometime during the 1840s, and local Indians reverentially gathered its acorns due to association with Serra. Several oaks are still claimed as descendants, most notably Monterey's Stokes Adobe oak at 500 Hartnell Street. On 3 June 1870, General Mariano Guadalupe Vallejo, born in Monterey in 1808, erected a wooden cross in front of the tree to commemorate the centennial of Monterey's founding. In 1889, a railroad embankment filled in part of the cove near the tree, shutting out the surf. A small stream near the tree no longer fed directly into the ocean, but via a culvert. With the widening of the road to Pacific Grove a few years later, the altered topography left the oak growing in a ditch and soon after 1900, the culvert collapsed and water backed up at its roots. On 6 July 1904, the *Monterey New Era* reported that the "living monument . . . was dead."[139] Shortly thereafter the tree was dug up and thrown into Monterey Bay by unsuspecting utilities workmen. San Carlos Pastor Reverend Ramón Mestres, learning this after it had "floated halfway to Santa Cruz," sent fishermen to harpoon and tow it back. In October 1905, the rotten trunk was "filled with concrete [as a new core] and a wire frame [was made to] hold trunk and branches . . . [which were] preserved with crude oil and creosote"[140] and placed on a pedestal for display behind San Carlos Church. A large Celtic Cross monument was erected at the tree's original location near the corner of Pacific and Artillery Streets in Monterey. As the twentieth-century progressed, the uncovered bark and branches slowly eroded from the cement frame and pieces were removed. The last remnants are now displayed in the vestibule of the church at 550 Church Street, Monterey.

65. Presidio-Mission San Carlos Borromeo's 3 June 1770 "founding document," inscribed by Serra on page one of that mission's *Libro de Bautismos*. The Spanish translates: "First book wherein are entered the Baptismal records of the gentiles who have become Christians of this Mission of San Carlos of the Port of Monterey which belongs to the Apostolic College *de Propaganda Fide* of San Fernando of Mexico, and is conducted by the missionaries of the Seraphic Order in so far as its spiritual needs are concerned. It was founded at the expense of our Catholic Monarch of both Spains, Lord Don Carlos III, whom God keep, and administered on the orders and full commission of the Most Excellent Lord Don Carlos Francisco de Croix, the Marquis de Croix, and present Viceroy and Captain General of this New Spain. [The founding was organized] by the Most Illustrious Lord Don Joseph de Gálvez, member of His Majesty's Council and Cabinet in the Royal and Supreme Council for the Indies, Superintendent of the Army and Inspector General of this New Spain. It is conducted by the Franciscan religious of the said Apostolic College, and was begun on the most solemn day, Pentecost Sunday, Feast of the Holy Spirit, on the third of June of the year 1770. Its first ministers were the Fathers Preachers Fray Junípero Serra, President, and Fray Juan Crespí, both sons of the holy Province of Majorca in Europe, and apostolic missionaries of the said Apostolic College of San Fernando of Mexico, for more than twenty years. This book contains 276 pages, not counting the first and last pages, which are blank." (Mission San Carlos Borromeo *Libro de Bautismos*, volume 1, recto 1, Diocese of Monterey Chancery Archives, Monterey)

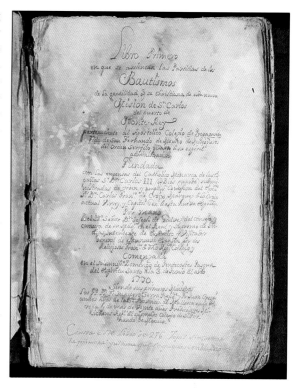

66. Monterey's *presidio*, where Serra lived from 4 June 1770 to 24 August 1771. Located eight-tenths of a mile inland from the Vizcaíno-Serra landing cove, the site was next to a salt water estuary, fresh water creek and an underground spring. Within an enclosed stockade of pine logs and earth, Serra's first Monterey church was one room in a three-room *jacal*, with the other two serving as priest quarters and warehouse. The mission itself, where the Indians lived and worked, was immediately outside the *presidio* walls. The compound was expanded (more in conformity with this 1791 view by José Cardero of the Spanish Malaspina Expedition) after Serra moved the mission aspect of the enterprise to Carmel in 1771. The enlarged *presidio* consisted of a fifty-*vara* square enclosed by *adobe* walls and a solid bank of one-story buildings around the perimeter. Within, a "Royal Presidio Chapel" with separate sacristy, several workshops, warehouses and living quarters. When Monterey replaced Loreto, Lower California as capital of Both Californias in 1777, Serra expressed his pleasure "at seeing our own Monterey, whose birth I witnessed, now made capital of so large a province."[141]

67. Monterey's Royal Presidio Chapel (known as San Carlos Church after American annexation in 1848, and as San Carlos Cathedral since 1967), built on the site of Serra's first Monterey church. He did not live to see construction of this building, designed and supervised by Mexico City's master stonemason Manuel Ruíz from 1792 to 1794. This is California's only remaining original *presidio* chapel and the sandstone figure of Our Lady of Guadalupe in the apex of the façade is California's oldest indigenous sculpture. (550 Church Street, Monterey)

68. Our Lady of Bethlehem statue. Devotion to the Virgin Mary as "Our Lady of Bethlehem" began among fifteenth-century Portuguese sailors who invoked the Blessed Mother's protection under the title *Nossa Senhora de Belém* (*Nuestra Señora de Belén* in Spanish). Mariner devotion grew and spread to Spain during the 1580-1640 dual monarchy, and then to the New World. This statue, owned by Most Reverend Francisco Antonio Lorenzana y Butrón, Archbishop of Mexico City from 1766 to 1771, was donated to the 'Sacred Expedition" to California in 1769 "so that it might go with the title *Conquistadora*"[142] (Our Lady of the Conquest). It was present at the founding of Presidio-Mission San Diego de Alcalá on 16 July 1769, and Presidio-Mission San Carlos Borromeo on 3 June 1770. Housed at Mission Carmel since 1771, it was mentioned several times by Serra and revered by Monterey's sailors. After the mission's abandonment in 1845, it was cared for by the last resident Indians and then several generations of Mexican families in Monterey. In December 1945, it was returned to the mission. Never retouched, the *encarnación* (porcelain-like gesso) matte-finish face and hands of the Mexican-made, early-eighteenth-century statue are in excellent condition. The glass eyes with real eyelashes are still intact. The Infant Jesus is original, as well as the inscribed silver crown, donated in thanksgiving in 1802 by a sailor who received special favor. The garments, although antique, were added in 1954. 62" tall. (Mission Carmel Basilica, Carmel)

69. Saint Joseph statue. Saint Joseph was chosen as patron of the Portolá-Serra Expedition as well as "titular patron" of Mission San Carlos Borromeo's church. Inspector General José de Gálvez, special agent of King Carlos III who organized the expedition, donated the statue for the mission's founding. It arrived on 31 May 1770 and was listed in the mission's 1770 founding *Inventario* as an "elaborate carved image of the Holy Patriarch Señor Saint Joseph."[143] Serra mentioned the statue in that mission's 1774 *Informe* after moving the mission to Carmel, wherein he noted a new "niche . . . of redwood for the holy image of Saint Joseph."[14] The statue was stored at Monterey's San Carlos Church during Carmel's abandonment (1852-1930), as were most of the mission's furnishings. Carved in Mexico in the mid-eighteenth century, the statue's face and hands maintain their original *encarnación* brilliant finish, and the tunic and mantle its *estofado* (lustrous stenciling) polychrome, 36" tall. (Mission Carmel Basilica, Carmel)

70. "Cloth of gold" vestments. Describing Serra as "that exemplary and zealous missionary," New Spain's Viceroy Carlos Francisco de Croix was "jubilant" when he learned that Monterey had finally been established. As a gift, and in response to Serra's 1770 request for "vestments of all sorts, sacred vessels for the churches, utensils for the houses and implements for the field,"[145] he donated several cases of church goods to the new enterprise, including this liturgical dalmatic, stole and appareled amice made from Chinese silk imported to Mexico via the Philippines. In thanking the viceroy on 18 June 1771, Serra wrote: "I received the complete vestments, especially chosen and the finest of all that came, by the generosity of Your Excellency as a gift to your favorite Mission of San Carlos de Monterey. I soon had the opportunity of showing it all of to advantage on the Solemnity of Corpus Christi that was not far off. We made a great event of it this year. . . . For your magnificent gift, I wish to return to Your Excellency all proper thanks, hoping that the Divine Majesty will reward you most abundantly for the help you have rendered."[146] 43" tall x 66" wide, stole 101" x 3." (Mission Carmel Museum, Carmel)

71. Serra's record of his first California Baptism, listed in Mission San Carlos Borromeo's *Libro de Bautismos.* Bernardino de Jesús, a Carmel Indian of the Rumsen ethnic group and the Costanoan linguistic group, was born in the Achista Ranchería, today part of Carmel proper. Since it was customary for the baptizing priest to confer a Christian name, Serra selected Saint Bernardine of Siena, namesake of his boyhood church/*convento* in Petra, and for the occasion Bernardino wore the "Brittany [linen] cap with lace and colored ribbons . . . [used] for Baptisms of small children."[147] Serra also confirmed Bernardino at Mission Carmel on 27 January 1779, and performed his marriage to Theresa de Jesús, another

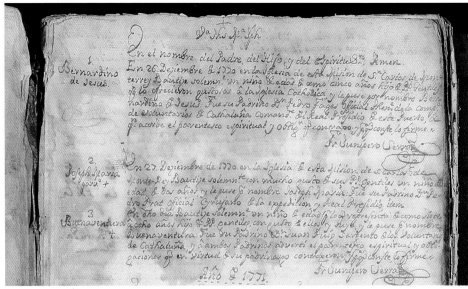

Christian Indian of the same *ranchería,* on 23 May 1780. Bernardino was present at Serra's funeral on 29 August 1784, and lived until 27 February 1792. The Spanish translates: "Hail Jesus, Mary, Joseph! (1) Bernardino de Jesús: In the name of the Father, of the Son, and of the Holy Spirit. Amen. On 26 December 1770, in the Church of this Mission of San Carlos de Monterey, I solemnly baptized a boy about five-years old, son of Gentile parents who willingly offered him to the Catholic Church, and I gave him the name Bernardino de Jesús. His godfather was Don Pedro Fages, Lieutenant Officer of the Catalan Company of Volunteers, Commandant of the Royal Presidio of this port, to whom I granted the spiritual bond and obligations that he assumed; and may it be recorded that I signed it. Fray Junípero Serra [rubric]." (Mission San Carlos Borromeo *Libro de Bautismos,* volume 1, recto 2, Diocese of Monterey Chancery Archives, Monterey)

72. First site of Mission San Antonio de Padua, where Serra established his third California mission. Somewhere on this broad, oak-dotted plain located about sixty miles southeast of Monterey, Serra selected a site near the San Antonio River for a new mission. Before the 14 July 1771 founding ceremony, he rang the bells suspended from the branch of a large oak and shouted: "Come you, pagans; come, come to the Holy Church; come, come to receive the Faith of Jesus Christ."[148] When reminded by fellow missionary and co-founder Father Miguel Pieras that not even one Indian was present, he replied: "Allow my overflowing heart to express itself. Would that this bell were heard throughout the world, as the Venerable Mother, Sister Mary of Agreda, desired it, or at least, that it were heard by every pagan who inhabits this area."[149] Serra was referring to Venerable Sister María de Jesús de Agreda (1602-65), a Spanish Poor Clare nun and mystic allegedly possessing the divine gifts of bilocation and tongues. Numerous Southwest American Indian and missionary accounts tell of her miraculous evangelical visitations from Spain to various Indian tribes, and of preaching in native tongues that paved the way for later Christian conversions. Her life and writings influenced Serra and his contemporaries, and copies of her book *Mística Ciudad de Dios (Mystical City of God,* published 1670) were always on hand at San Fernando College and in California mission libraries. Junípero Serra Peak, the highest point in the Santa Lucía Range of the Southern Coast Range (elevation 5,862 feet, name approved by the United States Geographic Board in 1907) is visible on the left. Against the hills on the right, the present Mission San Antonio. (One-half mile off Nacimiento-Ferguson Road, Fort Hunter Liggett, Jolon)

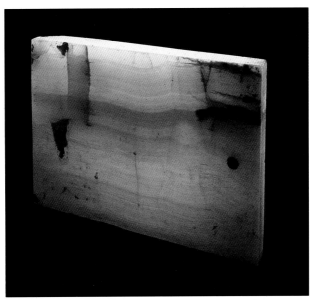

73. Puebla onyx altar stone, one of five requisitioned by Serra from Lower California and shipped to California in 1769. A small, hollowed-out circular sepulchrum (with seal intact) contains the necessary relics for creating a portable consecrated altar when the stone is placed on any table, perfect for use in the missionary field. 16-1/2" x 12" x 1-1/2" thick. (Mission Carmel Museum, Carmel)

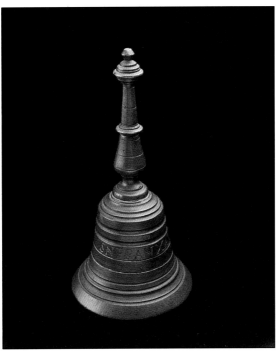

74. Bronze altar bell requisitioned by Serra from Mission San Francisco Xavier, Lower California and brought to California in 1769. The inscription reads: "SAN FRAN[co] XAVIEL." 5" tall x 2-1/2" diameter. (Mission Carmel Museum, Carmel)

75. Mission San Antonio de Padua at its present site, 2.5 miles southwest of the original. During the mission system's infancy, sites were changed according to improved knowledge of geography and climate, and buildings were replaced by progressively more sophisticated structures when material and manpower permitted. Such was the case at San Antonio, which was moved eighteen months after its founding because "the river dried up so that there was no more water . . . [so it was moved] farther up in the same valley to the banks of an *arroyo* ["stream," a tributary of the San Antonio River] . . . which, even in the driest time of the year, flows with . . . water."[150] Serra did not live to see the present church, completed in 1813. He visited the mission nine times, the first two at its original site and the remainder at the present one. (Mission Road, Fort Hunter Ligget, Jolon)

76. Mission San Antonio's 1776 tabernacle with *Ecce Homo* (Behold the Man, John 19:5), listed in that mission's 1776 *Informe*, and familiar to Serra when he visited Mission San Antonio. The painting, attributed to José de Paez, shows Jesus when introduced to the crowd after being scourged and crowned with thorns. The tabernacle was transferred to Monterey after San Antonio's abandonment in 1882, and to Mission Carmel in the 1950s. 32-1/2" x 23." (Mission Carmel Museum, Carmel)

77. *San Antonio de Padua*, selected by San Fernando College as namesake for Mission San Antonio de Padua. The painting was requested in a 1771 *Memoria* (*Account*, a request list) to San Fernando College, wherein Serra asked that "above all, [it be painted] with the Infant Jesus."[151] The painting, which cost eighteen *pesos*, was shipped to California during Serra's 1773 visit to Mexico City. Unaware of this, he commissioned another *San Antonio* while in Mexico, which he brought to San Diego by ship in 1774, and then overland to Mission San Antonio. San Antonio's missionaries accepted it as well, "kiss[ing], over and over again, their patron saint."[152] At least one of the paintings remained at San Antonio until 1882, when it was taken to Mission San Miguel. The other *San Antonio* is presumed lost. The oil on canvas is signed *"Jph. de Paez fecit en México"* (José de Paez executed this in Mexico). Saint Anthony of Padua (1195-1231, Portuguese Franciscan priest) wears Serra's gray San Fernando College habit, and halo. He holds the Infant Jesus in reference to a vision when the Child appeared to him. He also holds a lily, symbol of purity, and the book on the table refers to his title as *Doctor Evangelicus* (Evangelical Doctor) of the Church, for his great preaching and teaching authority. 38-1/2" x 58." (Mission San Miguel Church, San Miguel)

78. Replica of the founding cross Serra erected at Mission Carmel, at its original location within the mission's quadrangle, circa 1939. Mission San Carlos Borromeo, transplanted from Monterey on 24 August 1771, was thenceforth known as Misión San Carlos Borromeo del Río Carmelo (Mission Saint Charles Borromeo of the Carmel River) or simply as Mission Carmel. The name Carmel dated to 3 January 1603, when Sebastián Vizcaíno visited the area and named the bay, river and valley in honor of Our Lady of Mount Carmel, patroness of his Carmelite chaplains. Saint Charles Borromeo (1538-1584, Italian Third Order Franciscan cardinal bishop) was selected as patron of the mission by Inspector General José de Gálvez, in honor of the patron saint of both King Carlos III of Spain and Carlos Francisco de Croix, Viceroy of New Spain (no painting or statue of Saint Charles survives from Serra's period). Serra prayed daily in front of the cross "as soon as morning dawned" and at night when he "finished reciting the Franciscan Rosary [a seven-decade rosary signifying the Seven Joys of the Virgin Mary]."[153] In 1939, Mission Carmel Curator Harry Downie discovered the exact location of Serra's original cross: "While digging to put in a pepper tree, [he came across] several water-washed stones. . . . In mixed with the earth were small and dusty fragments of wood. . . . [He] knew that at last he had discovered the remnants of the first cross. . . . [He] built a new cross out of 10" x 10" squared hewn timbers from the mission itself [shown here, and which can be seen in the central courtyard today], . . . rising nearly fifteen feet. . . . Design of the cross, with its peculiar cap-piece, was copied from the engraving made by Sykes [of the 1792 English Vancouver Expedition]."[154]

79. Mission Carmel's seven churches, superimposed over a shaded floorplan of the compound at its peak, circa 1815 (which corresponds to the present layout): (1) Enramada Church of 24 August 1771 (an *enramada* is an arbor or bower, constructed of branches and brush); (2) Jacal Church of 1771-73 (a *jacal* is basically a hut, constructed of palisades, that is, poles/logs set upright in the ground, spaced three to four feet apart, interwoven with brush and with a tule roof); (3) Jacalón Church of 1773-78 (a *jacalón* is a larger, more elaborate *jacal*, which might substitute wood planks for brush, and beams plastered with mud for a tule roof); (4) Jacalón Grande Church of 1778-83; (5) Serra Adobe Church of 1783-93; (6) Provisional Church of 1793-97; (7) present Santa Lucía Sandstone Church.

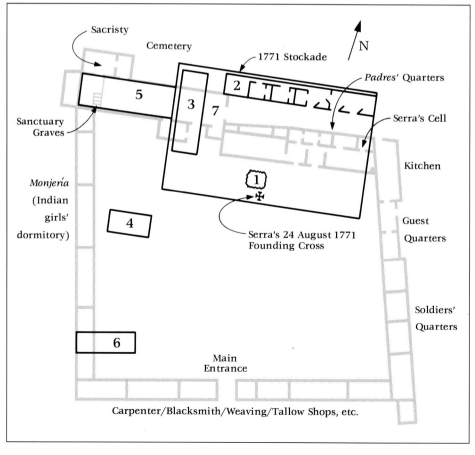

80. Basilica Mission San Carlos Borromeo del Río Carmelo, headquarters of the California mission chain and residence of the *padre-presidente*. Serra lived here from 24 August 1771 until his death on 28 August 1784. He did not live to see the present stone church, the seventh on approximately the same site, dedicated in September 1797. However, portions of the north and east wings of the *adobe* quadrangle, constructed in 1778, and now incorporated into the restored museum wing and Blessed Sacrament Chapel, date from his period. (3080 Rio Road, Carmel)

81. Serra's Mission Carmel *celdilla* (cell). In this small room (11'9" x 11'7"), Serra died just before 2 p.m. on Saturday 28 August 1784. After the mission was abandoned in 1852, the room fell into ruin, and by the time it was restored in 1937, only the foundation and first few feet of wall remained. Curator Harry Downie used original materials and floor tiles gathered from other parts of the compound to reconstruct it. The dedication ceremony took place on 29 August 1937, when, after a Solemn High Mass, the cell was blessed by Reverend Augustine Hobrecht, O.F.M., first Serra Cause vice-postulator. He delivered a speech about Serra's "life and labors" and members of the Onesimo family, the last Mission Carmel Indians, placed a wreath and flowers on the replica bed. Afterward, "as a happy and blessed ending to the day, Solemn Benediction of the Blessed Sacrament . . . was given at the grave of Father Serra."[155] The replica bed, constructed from original mission timbers, follows Francisco Palóu's description: "His bed consisted of some roughhewn boards, covered by a blanket serving more as a covering than an aid to rest for he never used even a sheepskin cover, as was customary."[156] The only authentic Serra artifact in the room is the *disciplina* hanging on the wall, and possibly the Bible on the table.

82. Serra's Bible? This vellum-covered Bible, printed in Lyons, France in 1568, is not signed by Serra. However, the half-title page is missing, the most likely place for inscriptions. One unclear signature appears on the title page along with *ex libris* (from the library of) and a partial 1780s date. There are several internal Latin inscriptions, but none in Serra's hand. The book is not marked "property of San Fernando College," but this was not strictly required until 1809. Therefore, it is impossible to prove this was indeed Serra's Bible. Nevertheless, local tradition strongly suggests that he personally brought it from Loreto, Lower California to San Diego in 1769, to Monterey in 1770, and to Mission Carmel in 1771. When Ronald Reagan used this Bible to swear his first-term oath of office as California governor on 2 January 1967, it was described as a "Bible brought to California by famed Spanish missionary Father Junípero Serra, now housed permanently [at] Carmel Mission. . . . "It is to my knowledge, the oldest Bible in California," said Harry Downie, curator at the Carmel Mission."[157] 1,240 pages. 7-1/2" x 5-1/2" x 2-1/2" thick. (Mission Carmel Museum, Carmel)

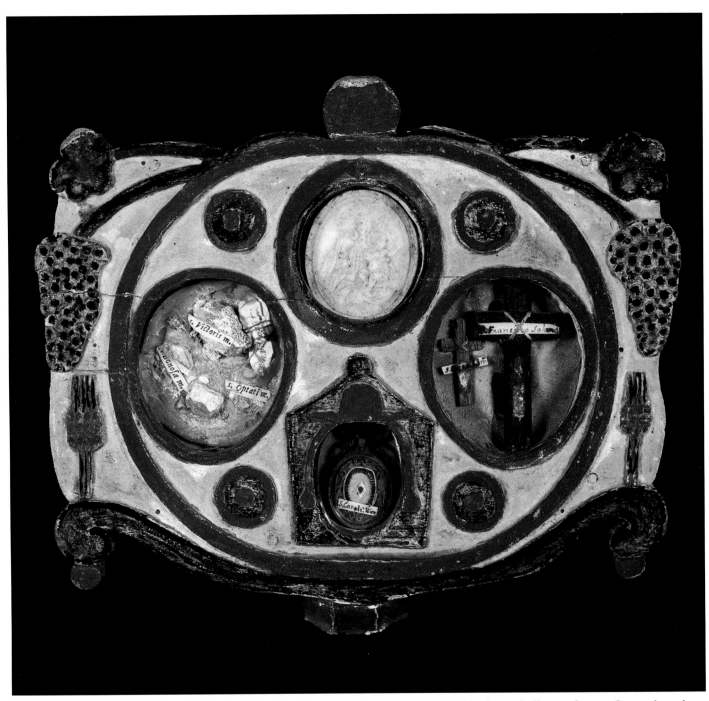

83. Detail from Serra's Indian reliquary, traditionally believed to have been made for him by an Indian craftsman. It may have been copied from another reliquary or engraving, since the design is not aboriginal. A faded, barely decipherable description of the contents is on the reverse side, which a court-certified documents and handwriting expert verified was written by Serra. Bordered in front with carved wheat and grapes representing the bread and wine of the Eucharist, the relics under glass are (clockwise from top): (1) wax *Agnus Dei* (Lamb of God) sacramental of Our Lady of the Rosary and Infant Jesus, issued during the pontificate of Pius VI (1775-99). A sacramental is a "sacred sign which resembles the Sacraments," such as holy water, rosaries or an *Agnus Dei. Agnus Dei's* are blessed by the Pope on Holy Wednesday in the first and successive seventh years of his pontificate and distributed on Holy Saturday, a tradition dating from the fourth century as protection against natural disaster; (2) bone, habit and wood from the grave of Saint Francis Solano, Apostle of South America and Serra's favorite saint (large cross), and bone and wood from the grave of Saint Rose of Lima, Patroness of South America (small cross); (3) *púrpura* (scarlet-red cardinal's cloth) relic of Saint Charles Borromeo, namesake of Mission Carmel church, within decorative carved church and cardinal's hat; (4) bones of early Christian martyrs set in wax. 10" x 8" x 1-3/4" thick, 19-1/4" tall with base. (Mission Carmel Museum, Carmel)

84. Silver "True Cross" reliquary. This unmarked, mid-eighteenth-century cross was sent to California from Mexico City in 1774, donated by San Fernando College as a gift to the mission enterprise. Serra described it in Mission Carmel's 1774 *Informe* as a "silver cross with its pedestal of the same metal, more than a third of a *vara*, with its *lingum crucis auténtico* [authentic True Cross relic] . . . in a little crystal crosspiece."[158] The relic described by Serra fit into the crosspiece, now covered with a small panel decorated with flowers and circles. This was added in 1930, after the original relic and glass had disappeared. At that time, an oval incision was made in the hollow stem and a second True Cross relic was added. The three-sided base depicts: (1) First Order Franciscan coat of arms (shown here); (2) "Santiago Matamoros" (Saint James the Greater as "Moorslayer"), patron of Spain; (3) The *Cinco Llagas* depicted as five hearts. The *repoussé*-decorated cross weighs 23 ounces Troy. 15" tall x 6-3/4" base diameter, 7-1/2" at crosspiece. (Mission Carmel Museum, Carmel)

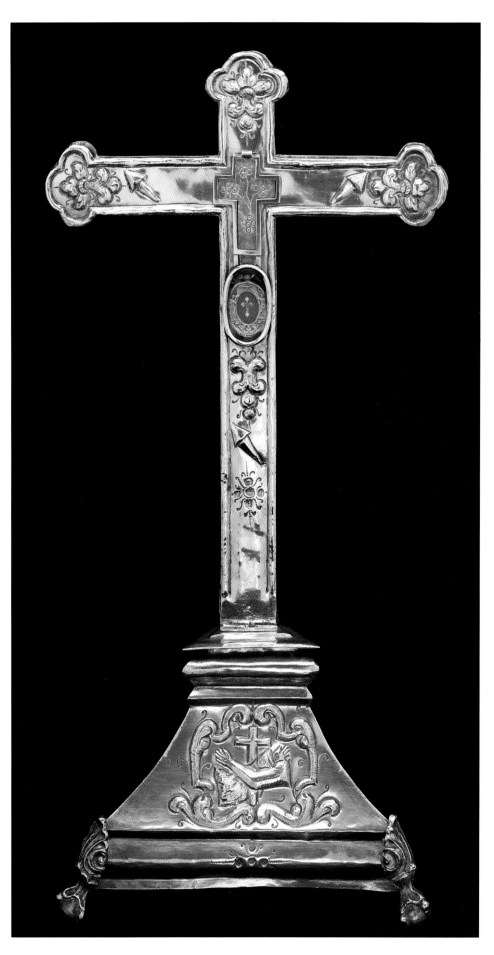

85. *La Gloria* (The Glory of Heaven) painting ordered by Serra from Mexico City in a 1771 Mission Carmel *Memoria*, along with a now lost Horrors of Hell companion. The paintings arrived in 1774, and are listed in that mission's 1774 *Informe* as "new additions to Church and sacristy."[159] They were hung in the body of the church and in 1787, California's first "foreign" visitor, Frenchman Jean François de Galaup, Comte de la Pérouse, found the Horrors of Hell "absolutely necessary to appeal to the senses of [the] recent converts," but thought the Glory of Heaven "too sublime for [them] to comprehend."[160] The Glory portrays the Trinity, Mary and Joseph, a number of Biblical figures, saints and martyrs. Of particular note are Saint Francis of Assisi kneeling on the right, wearing a gray San Fernando College habit holding a cross and with his left hand outstretched to his contemporary and friend Saint Dominic, representing camaraderie between the Franciscan and Dominican Orders. The painting is signed "*Jphs. de Paez fecit, en México*" (José de Paez executed this, in Mexico). 77" 60." (Mission Carmel Basilica, Carmel)

86. Silver Bucareli Monstrance. "Willing to buy it with the blood of his own veins"[161] if necessary, Serra requested a new monstrance from Viceroy Bucareli by letter on 27 June 1776. When it arrived at Monterey on 31 July 1778, he exclaimed: "Our joy was great when we took off the coverings and looked and looked at it with wondering eyes. Everyone was highly delighted."[162] Serra blessed and first used it to hold the consecrated Host on Sunday 9 August 1778. The monstrance, the best documented Serra artifact in California, is inscribed in Spanish at its base: "Belonging to Carmel Mission in New California, donated by the Most Excellent Lord Knight Commander Don Antonio Bucareli y Ursúa, Viceroy of New Spain, and in the year 1777." It is made of Mexican silver with a gilt finish. The detachable *custodia* (custody) is incised and decorated with applied cherubs and the scalloped base and stem with *repoussé*. The underside is stamped with three hallmarks: (1) GOSALEZ, mark of Mexico's chief assayer from 1731 to 1778, Captain of Grenadiers Diego González de la Cueva; (2) crowned "M" Mexican tax mark; (3) eagle on cactus signifying quality and purity of the metal. 70 ounces Troy. 24" tall x 9-1/4" base diameter. (Mission Carmel Museum, Carmel)

87. *Nuestra Señora de los Dolores* (Our Lady of Sorrows) painting ordered by Serra for Mission Carmel in 1776. When it arrived from Mexico City in 1778, he noted that it was placed in the sanctuary of the church above a special "altar [with its] curtains, etc., [and it is] very devotional."[163] Serra was buried at the foot of this altar in the fifth "Serra Adobe" Church. The painting commemorates Mary's sorrows during her Son's life and death, hence the dagger in her heart. Jesus is shown with symbols of the Passion at His feet, assisted by Saint John the Apostle and Saint Mary Magdalene. The painting, signed *"Ma Rodríguez pinxit a 1777"* (Martín [or possibly Miguel] Rodríguez painted this in 1777), was restored in the 1930s and still hangs in its original frame. 70" x 61" with frame. (Mission Carmel Basilica, Carmel)

88. Mexican-cedar and California-redwood confessional constructed at Mission Carmel after the cedar was shipped from Mexico City. It is mentioned in that mission's 1779 *Informe* as a new "confessional of redwood, with its seat of the same wood."[164] 74" tall x 30" x 26." (Mission Carmel Museum, Carmel)

89. *San Juan de la Crus* (Saint John of the Cross) bell. Seven tower bells were originally requisitioned from Lower California's missions for California in 1769, all since lost. This is Mission Carmel's earliest remaining bell, inscribed 1781, and therefore present during Serra's last year or two. It was cast in Mexico with a three-eyeleted handle and diamond-shaped cross above the inscription. 20" tall x 19" diameter. (Mission Carmel belltower, Carmel)

90. Mission San Gabriel Arcángel, California's fourth. Serra was not present at the mission's founding by Fathers Ángel Somera and Pedro Cambón on 8 September 1771, nor did he live to see the present church, completed in 1805. The mission was originally located five miles south of the present one near the Río Hondo (San Gabriel and Lincoln Avenues, Montebello). It was moved near the San Gabriel River in May 1775, to a "location [that] is very good. It has an oak grove quite close which is very advantageous for obtaining timber and firewood, and is within sight of a great plain where the soil is not the best quality for in part it is very sandy and rocky, but with the irrigating ditch . . . [it] will fructify."[165] Selected by New Spain's Viceroy Croix, the name honors the Archangel Gabriel (no known painting or statue of Gabriel survives from Serra's period). Serra visited the mission seven times, the first two at the original site, where on 19 April 1774, he performed his first California wedding and the state's first Caucasian one, and the remainder at the present one. (537 West Mission Drive, San Gabriel)

91. Mission San Gabriel's *Nuestra Señora de los Dolores*. This image played a decisive role in pacifying San Gabriel's hostile Indians, for when the canvas was unfurled they "were conquered by that beautiful image. They threw down their bows and arrows and the two chiefs rushed forward to place at the feet of the Sovereign Queen the beads they wore around their necks, as gifts of great esteem."[166] Little is known of the painting's provenance, most likely late-seventeenth-century Mexican. The approximately 20" x 24" canvas remained at Mission San Gabriel until it was stolen from the sanctuary in 1977. The photograph is from the original.

92. Mission San Luís Obispo de Tolosa, California's fifth, founded by Serra on 1 September 1772. He did not live to see the present church, completed in 1794. He chose a site in the "Valley of the Bears . . . with good lands for crops, through which ran a clear *arroyo* to water them [San Luís Obispo Creek]."[167] After the founding, he left behind "only two *arrobas* [one Spanish *arroba* equals 25.4 pounds] of flour and three *almudes* [one Spanish *almud* equals two-tenths of a bushel] of wheat. And in order that [the resident missionary] might be able to buy seeds from the pagan Indians, he left them a box of brown sugar."[168] Serra later commented that the meager circumstances of its founding were considered "rash" by all, but that "he who trusts in [God] shall not be confounded."[169] The mission, never relocated, was visited by Serra seven times. (Monterey and Chorro Streets, San Luis Obispo)

93. *San Luís Obispo*, selected by San Fernando College as namesake of Mission San Luís Obispo. Serra ordered the painting in 1771, asking that Saint Louis be portrayed with "the Franciscan habit and cord plainly to be seen."[170] The painting was one of *two* San Luís Obispo's shipped from Mexico in 1774. As with the *San Antonio de Padua* painting, Serra mistakenly ordered a second while in Mexico in 1773, but San Luís' priests did *not* want the second one he brought back by land. Serra thought it the "nicer executed" of the two and took it on to Mission Carmel. It is difficult to say which survives today, since they were similar. Mission Carmel shows receipt of one in 1774, but it does not appear in its 1834 or 1842 secularization inventories. Mission San Luís Obispo's early records are missing, but it does show one in its 1857 secularization inventory. Whether this is the original, or Carmel's misplaced portrait that Serra thought the "nicer" of the two may never be known. The unsigned oil on canvas is attributed to José de Paez. Saint Louis of Anjou, Bishop of Toulouse (1274-1297, French-Hungarian Franciscan bishop) is shown with episcopal insignia over a gray San Fernando College habit and faint halo. The crown and scepter in the foreground refer to the throne of Naples and Sicily he renounced to become a Franciscan, the basket of bread in the background to his apostolate among the poor, and the book on the table to his episcopate. 55-1/2" x 38-1/4." (Mission San Luís Obispo Church, San Luis Obispo)

S. LUIS OBISPO.

94. Church and Apostolic College of Santa Cruz de Querétaro, Querétaro, Mexico, situated at the crossroads to the northern Sierra Gorda missionary field and the western supply route from Mexico City to the Pacific coast port of San Blas. Serra stayed here whenever he went back and forth, including during his years as a Sierra Gorda missionary and when he visited Mexico City for the last time in 1773. Founded by Majorcan Antonio Llinás in 1683, Santa Cruz was the mother college of all Franciscan apostolic colleges in the New World. The bronze statue of Serra, commissioned by the city of Querétaro, was dedicated in 1984. He is depicted wearing a Caravaca cross, with pick and shovel in hand, and standing next to a cornstalk and basket of wheat. (Avenida Venustiano Carranza, Querétaro)

95. Entrance to New Spain's viceregal palace (now Mexico's National Palace), through which Serra passed in early March 1773 to confer with Viceroy Bucareli. Antonio María Bucareli y Ursúa, born of noble lineage in Seville, Spain, served as forty-sixth viceroy of New Spain from 22 September 1771 until his death on 9 April 1779. His 5,000,000-square-mile viceroyalty, stretching from Guatemala in the south to roughly Oregon and across to Louisiana in the north, consisted of a vast administrative network of kingdoms, provinces, presidencies, judicial divisions and local governments. (East side of the Plaza Mayor, Mexico City)

96. Mexico City's former archiepiscopal palace, where Juan Evangelista, a Mission Carmel Indian boy, became the first California native to receive the Sacrament of Confirmation. On the left, the twin towers of Mexico City's cathedral, where "a general ringing of bells at the cathedral and all the other churches in the capital"[171] was ordered when news reached Mexico City that Monterey had been founded on 3 June 1770. Juan Evangelista José, born in the Ichxenta Ranchería on Carmel Bay near Point Lobos, was baptized and named by Serra at age nine on 19 March 1771. He accompanied Serra to Mexico city in 1773, and although very ill en route, once recovered he "won the attention of all."[172] Serra arranged for him to be confirmed by Most Reverend Alfonso Núñez de Haro y Peralta, Archbishop of Mexico City, in the private chapel of his residence on 4 August 1773. After returning to California, Juan shared the highlights of his Mexican

sojourn with his people and began re-educating them. For example, they were "rid of their belief that the Spaniards are the offspring of mules, a notion they previously had, seeing that mules were the only members of the female gender they saw among us."[173] In September 1774, the Indians harvested sardines from among great schools that appeared in Carmel Bay and in the name of his people, Juan sent Viceroy Bucareli a barrel of the salted, dried fish. Serra hoped that "his present, although a poor one, will nonetheless be appreciated,"[174] and indeed, ten months later Juan received a thank-you note from the viceroy. Serra officiated at Juan's wedding on 2 December 1775 when he married Thomasa María, also from his *ranchería*. The couple made their home at the mission but died young, for on 9 August 1778, Serra wrote: "My poor Juan died on the ninth day after his wife [both from measles], after receiving all the Sacraments, and I buried him in our habit [he was a Third Order Franciscan]."[175] On 27 December of the same year, Serra baptized a baby boy, born the same day in the Ichxenta Ranchería, and in memoriam, named him Juan Evangelista. (Calles Moneda and Seminario, Mexico City)

97. San Antonio *regalito* (little gift), presented by Serra to Lieutenant José Francisco Ortega upon Serra's return from Mexico in 1774. Ortega, a Mexican career soldier, first met Serra in his capacity as official scout for the 1769 Portolá-Serra Expedition. When Serra returned aboard the *Santiago*, the ship carried food and supplies for the missions, art work and church goods, and undoubtedly a number of personal items procured by Serra for fellow missionaries and friends. He presented Ortega, then San Diego Presidio military commandant, with two small *regalitos*, which were treasured by six generations of Ortegas. The tiny polychromed wooden figure of Saint Anthony of Padua, wearing a brown Franciscan habit, holds the Infant Jesus and a loaf of bread (symbolic of his role as "Apostle of Charity"). The eighteenth-century carving is housed in a fourteen-piece, handmade niche, possibly a later addition made in California. 2-1/2" tall statue, 7-3/4" with niche. (Santa Barbara Mission Archive-Library, Santa Barbara)

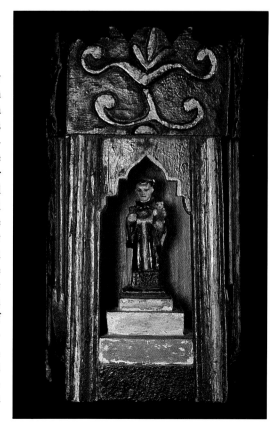

98. *Madre Dolorosa* (Sorrowful Mother) *regalito* presented by Serra to Lieutenant José Francisco Ortega in 1774. Small devotional items like this framed print, easily transported to the frontier, were once common in California. The hand-colored engraving is probably Spanish eighteenth-century. The frame, carved from a single piece of wood, is probably Mexican in origin. The off-center hole for hanging and the crudely-cut original glass suggest a mass-produced, albeit handmade item. 6-3/4" x 5" with frame. (Santa Barbara Mission Archive-Library, Santa Barbara)

99. Mission San Francisco de Asís, California's sixth. Serra was not present at the founding on 9 October 1776, officiated by Francisco Palóu, nor did he live to see the present church, completed in 1791. Named after Saint Francis of Assisi, his name was reserved for the northernmost mission founded during Serra's presidency (no known painting or statue of Saint Francis survives from Serra's period). Serra first asked Inspector General José de Gálvez for a mission named after his Order's patron in 1767, and Gálvez is to have replied: "If Saint Francis desires a mission in his honor, let him see to it that his port is located, and his name shall be given to it."[176] At that time, present San Francisco Bay lay undiscovered, and Gálvez was referring to "old" San Francisco Bay (present Drake's Bay, just north of San Francisco), familiar through previous explorer's records. When Serra visited San Francisco for the first time in October 1777 (accidentally discovered by the 1769 Portolá Expedition in search of Monterey Bay), he exclaimed: "Thanks be to God. Now Our Father Saint Francis, the crossbearer in the procession of missions, has come to the final point on the mainland of California; for in order to go

farther on, ships will be necessary."[177] Mission San Francisco was originally located 1,100 feet east of its present site, near the shore of Arroyo de los Dolores (Stream of the [Seven] Dolors [of the Virgin Mary]). Palóu moved it away from the small, now dry lakebed in 1783, since that area was agriculturally more valuable. Serra visited the mission four times, the first at its original site (nine city blocks between Guerrero and Howard, 15th and 20th Streets) and the last time at its present one. (Dolores and 16th Streets, San Francisco)

100. Mission San Francisco altar silver. The ciborium was one of two present at the mission's founding, a "gift from the King . . . of silver with its two covers."[178] The silver missal stand, not listed, was a later gift from another mission. Serra donated the "large and serviceable" monstrance to San Francisco in August 1778, after he received the Bucareli Monstrance for Mission Carmel. It had been at Carmel since its founding, listed in the original 1770 *Inventario* as "one silver-gilt monstrance with its cases."[179] All three pieces remained at San Francisco until 1982, when the missal stand and monstrance were stolen. The originals are shown here, circa 1930.

101. *El Palo Alto* (The Tall Timber) circa 1880, one of the last natural landmarks along California's original El Camino Real. Located on the south bank of San Francisquito Creek in the present city of Palo Alto, the 1,000-year-old *sequoia sempervirens* (coast redwood) was first used as a reference point by the 1769 Portolá Expedition that discovered San Francisco Bay, which measured it at 135 feet tall. Serra passed the redwood each time he visited Mission San Francisco, and it is still living minus one trunk that fell in 1886. In 1906, the Camino Real Association erected 450 cast-iron replica mission bells along the original El Camino as "distinctive, emblematic and appropriate guideposts."[180] (Alma and Palo Alto Streets, Palo Alto)

102. Mission San Juan Capistrano, California's seventh, circa 1895. The Serra Chapel, shown here, where Serra administered the Sacraments, is actually the mission's fourth church, at its second and present site. In the photograph, it is viewed with recently restored roof from its east side, next to the ruins of the stone church to its left. San Juan Capistrano was originally established two miles northeast of the present site, on the opposite bank of San Juan Creek (at San Juan Creek Road and Camino Lacouague, San Juan Capistrano). The founding, hastily postponed after Mission San Diego was burned in 1775, finally transpired on 1 November 1776. Serra "unearthed the bells [buried the year before for protection], at the peal of which, the pagans gathered, very glad to see that the fathers had returned to their territory."[181] Serra visited the original site twice, on the 1-3 November 1776 founding, and again later that month until 6 December, after a short trip to Mission San Gabriel to gather supplies for the new mission. In October 1778, all operations were moved to the present site (at 31414 Camino Capistrano, San Juan Capistrano) in search of a better water supply from Trabuco Creek. The first church at the present site, actually the mission's third church, was also considered temporary, and built immediately outside the perimeter of the southwest corner of the present quadrangle near the ruins of the stone church. The fourth church, the "Serra Chapel," was planned as more permanent and constructed entirely of *adobe* along the quadrangle's east wing. First mentioned in the mission's 1782 *Informe*, it was described as "a church, 25 x 7 *varas*, with its sacristy 6 x 7 *varas*. The walls were two *adobes* thick, covered by a flat *jacal* roof, to keep the water out. The main entrance faced the patio."[182] Serra visited the mission twice at this location to administer Confirmation: on 21-30 October 1778, in the temporary third church; and on 9-16 October 1783, to celebrate Mass and administer Confirmation "in this [adobe] church of the Mission of San Juan Capistrano or Quanissavit [the Serra Chapel]." As listed in his personal *Libro de Confirmaciones* (*Book of Confirmations*), Serra confirmed "ninety *párvulos* [young children] on Sunday 12 October, 123 on Monday, 7 on Tuesday and 1 on Wednesday."[183] He left San Juan Capistrano for the last time on 16 October. In 1790, the chapel's roof was removed. The walls were raised five *cuartas* (one Spanish *cuarta* equals eight linear inches) and the building enlarged. New roof timbers were installed, and the entire structure covered with tile. This is today's Serra Chapel, which continued in use until 1806, when the fifth and final "great stone church" was completed. After its earthquake-induced collapse in 1812, the chapel was once again pressed into service for the remainder of the mission period, which may account for its survival. The chapel fell into ruin after 1834, part of its roof collapsed in the 1850s, and it was abandoned for a time in the 1880s. Around 1895 it was reroofed and cleaned, and by 1922 its interior largely restored. Therefore, it may be stated that a portion of this chapel is the only extant structure in California within which Serra said Mass and administered the Sacraments. The two sections are distinguishable by examining the texture and consistency of *adobe* in the chapel's long east wall. In the photograph, there is one pattern on the lower right half, and another on the left half with panhandle that surmounts the right half. The shorter, older portion on the right is all that remains of Serra's "Serra Chapel."

103. West side of Mission San Juan Capistrano's Serra Chapel. The left half dates from Serra's period.

104. Interior of Mission San Juan Capistrano's Serra Chapel. Serra was familiar with the half closest to the altar, seventy-five feet from the *reredos* (installed in 1922) to the middle of the church where an irregular impression in the plastered, painted *adobe* wall delineates the two phases of construction. Everything from that point to the front door, forty-five more feet, was added in 1790. With its width limited by the size of available trees for ceiling beams, the overall interior measures 120 feet long by 18 feet wide, with 4 foot thick walls.

SAN JUAN CAPISTRANO.

105. *San Juan Capistrano*, selected by New Spain's Viceroy Bucareli as namesake for Mission San Juan Capistrano. Serra requested a patron saint painting for the mission in 1775, asking that the saint "have a handsome, resolute and devout appearance."[184] The painting, which cost twenty *pesos*, arrived in time for the mission's founding and has remained there since. Saint John Capistran (1386-1456, Italian Franciscan priest) is depicted with breastplate over a gray San Fernando College habit, and sword and cross-tipped banner emblazoned with IHS. This refers to his Crusades against the "infidel," most notably against the Turks at Belgrade in 1465, which is credited with sparing the siege of Christian Europe. The birds in the background refer to "souls" he helped save. The painting is signed "*Jph de Paez fecit, en México*" (José de Paez executed this, in Mexico). 40-1/2" x 31-1/2." (Mission San Juan Capistrano Parish Church, San Juan Capistrano)

106. Cross and park commemorating the third Mission Santa Clara de Asís (with the church's original foundation delineated around the park's perimeter at Franklin Street and El Camino Real), which Serra dedicated on 15 May 1784. Serra was not present at the 12 January 1777 founding of California's eighth mission by Fathers José Murguía and Tomás de la Peña at its original site "in the fertile lowlands of the River of Our Lady of Guadalupe"[185] (at De La Cruz Boulevard and Central Expressway, Santa Clara). Serra visited the first mission twice during 1777: from 28 September to 1 October, during his first tour of the "northern missions," and again on 9-10 October en route back to Carmel. In January 1779, the mission was moved about one-half mile south to higher ground to avoid flooding (at De La Cruz Boulevard and Martin Avenue, Santa Clara). Serra visited the second mission four times: from 11-14 October 1779, en route to San Francisco, and on 6-17 November to administer Confirmation on the way back to Mission Carmel; on 24 October 1781, en route to San Francisco, and 8-19 November to administer Confirmation on the way back. At that time, he blessed the cornerstone for a new, more permanent *adobe* church and mission that was to be built at a third site about one mile south of the second one (at Franklin Street and El Camino Real, Santa Clara). Serra returned from 29 April to 4 May 1784, went to San Francisco, and returned to Santa Clara on 15 May to dedicate the finished church. Joy and mourning intermingled because, although the new *adobe* church was to be dedicated, its principal builder, Father José Murguía, a friend of Serra's since their Sierra Gorda days, had died suddenly on 11 May. He was buried in the sanctuary of "the most beautiful church yet erected in California."[186] Serra officiated at the dedication on 15-16 May, one of his final public appearances, and departed on 24 May for the last time. The church was used until 1812, when earthquake damage forced abandonment and relocation of the entire compound, this time 1,600 feet to the southwest where the present mission stands. The original founding cross blessed by Serra on 19 November 1781 was also moved, and a portion is encased in a protective sheath in front of the present church. Mission Santa Clara is the only one of Serra's nine California missions definitely known to have been moved to an entirely new site *after* his death.

107. Cornerstone, crucifix and medals from Mission Santa Clara's third church, blessed by Serra on 19 November 1781. As recorded in the mission's *Libro de Bautismos*, "a cross, images and several coins, [which symbolize] the Church treasury,"[187] were placed in the cavity of the stone. At its original location and with contacts intact, the cornerstone was accidentally unearthed on 8 June 1911 by workmen digging for a gas main along Franklin Street near Campbell Avenue (now El Camino Real) in Santa Clara. "The opening was covered by a common cobblestone of a size to fit, but did not seal the opening. . . . The contents of the stone had been wrapped in some sort of silk fabric which disintegrated with handling and exposure to the air."[188] Within were found: a small bronze crucifix with an image of the Virgin Mary on the reverse (shown here in the cavity); a bronze medal with Saint Francis of Assisi on one side and Saint Anthony of Padua and the Infant Jesus on the other (show here); a bronze medal with Saint Joseph and the Infant Jesus on one side and Our Lady of Solitude on the other (shown here); and eight Spanish coins of the period. 15" x 12" x 8." (de Saisset Museum, Santa Clara University, Santa Clara)

108. Santa Clara de Asís, chosen by New Spain's Viceroy Bucareli as namesake for Mission Santa Clara. Saint Clare of Assisi (1194-1253, Italian nun and foundress of the Poor Clares) was a contemporary of Saint Francis of Assisi, and the first woman chosen as namesake of a California mission. Two Saint Clare statues appear in the mission's early records, one arriving in 1778, the other in 1782. The second one, fifty inches tall and more elaborate, was most likely the one placed above the main altar. Therefore, the statue shown here, preserved when the mission was moved to its present site in 1812 with *reredos* intact, was present on 15 May 1784 when Serra dedicated the third Mission Santa Clara Church. The church burned in 1926, and a replica statue has replaced the original. Saint Clare (the original is shown here, circa 1910) wears the habit of her Order and holds a monstrance and staff. The monstrance refers to her devotion to the Holy Eucharist, which helped liberate the city of Assisi from the Muslims in 1240, and the crosier to her role as abbess and foundress.

109. Serra's leatherbound, Mission Carmel *Libro de Confirmaciones*. Each mission had a set of "spiritual result" registers, as described by Serra in 1771: "Each mission received from me . . . two blank registers, well bound and lined in reddish sheepskin for the registration of Baptisms and burials, the two things that are first likely to occur."[189] In addition to the *Libro de Bautismos* (*Book of Baptisms*) and *Libro de Difuntos* (*Book of Deaths*), each mission eventually received a *Libro de Casamientos* (*Book of Marriages*), a *Libro de Confirmaciones* (*Book of Confirmations*) and some a *Libro de Cuentas* (*Book of Expenses*). Serra used Mission Carmel's *Libro de Confirmaciones* as a master record of all Confirmations he performed from 29 June 1778 to 6 July 1784, a total of 5,308. 12" x 9" x 1" thick. (Diocese of Monterey Chancery Archives, Monterey)

110. Serra's handwritten record of his first Confirmation and the first within California, administered at Mission Carmel on 29 June 1778. He confirmed a seven-year-old Indian boy, the son of the local chief, along with eighty-nine other young Indians. The boy's Christian name was Junípero Bucareli, selected by Serra when he baptized him four years prior. He lists the young Junípero as number two, having recorded Juan Evangelista's Mexico City Confirmation as number one. The Spanish translates: "Jesus, Mary and Joseph. In the name of Jesus Christ, Amen. On 29 June 1778, in the Church of the Mission of San Carlos de Monterey belonging to the Apostolic College of San Fernando of Mexico and to the Minor Order of Our Holy Father Saint Francis, after attending to the formalities noted at the beginning of this book, I the undersigned Fray Junípero Serra, vested in the same priestly vestments in which I had just finished singing Mass on that solemn day, dedicated to the Holy Apostles Saint Peter and Saint Paul, and assisted by Fray Juan Crespí and Fray Francisco Dumetz, both of them Apostolic Fathers of the College and co-Ministers of this Mission, with the newest chrism to be had, prepared and blessed by the Right Reverend Lord Bishop of Guadalajara, [I] solemnly confirmed according to the Roman Ritual, the following: (2) Junípero Bucareli: First, I confirmed the child Junípero, of about seven years of age, the legitimate son of Antonio María Bucareli, at that time Chief of the heathendom of these parts, and María Antonina Ursúa. The parents were a newly baptized couple from the Ichxenta Ranchería, called by us San José. The child's godfather was Fernando Chamorro, a Mexican, married, and a blacksmith for Our Lord the King of these Missions." (Mission San Carlos Borromeo *Libro de Confirmaciones*, recto 3, Diocese of Monterey Chancery Archives, Monterey)

111. *San Juan Bautista*, one of the most popular California mission art themes and educational tools, showing Jesus at the moment he received Baptism from Saint John the Baptist. The portable *lienzo de enrollar* (roll-up canvas) with hinged wooden tube at the top that opened to accept the rolled canvas, was perfect for the missionary field. Once closed and hooked, the painting was travel safe. Since Mission San Luís Obispo's early records are missing, it is impossible to ascertain its exact arrival date at that mission, although the painting does appear in the mission's 1857 post-secularization inventory. Saint John is shown holding a staff with cross entwined with a Latin banner declaring: "Behold [the] Lamb of God, Behold [Him] Who takes away the sins" (John 1:29). God the Father with faint triangular halo and God the Holy Spirit with aureole look on from above. The painting is signed "*Jph. de Paez fecit, en México a. v 1775*" (José de Paez executed this, in Mexico in the year 1775). 34-3/4" x 25." (Mission San Luís Obispo sacristy, San Luis Obispo)

112. *San Juan Bautista*, ordered by Serra for Mission Carmel in 1776, and arrived in 1777. This near duplicate of the left *Bautista* illustrates the "open stock" concept of mission art as less than the unique works generally assumed. Orders were often filled by San Fernando College's syndic from stock on hand at various Mexico City studios, and then shipped to the California missions. When compared with the previous *Bautista*, one sees the same theme, figures and composition, but with a number of minor variations and additions. Cherubs look on from high, birds perch in the tree and several in flight adorn the background. The animals and birds are symbolic, for example the hare, a defenseless creature, represents mankind who must put his hope of salvation in Jesus and His Passion. The unsigned painting by José de Paez matches two more unsigned Paez *Bautistas* at Missions San Buenaventura and San Miguel, both with sparingly applied embellishments. 31-1/2" x 39-1/2." (Mission Carmel Basilica, Carmel)

113. Mission San Buenaventura, California's ninth, and Serra's tenth and last. Serra did not live to see the present church, completed in 1809. Founded by Serra on 31 March 1782, it was located just south of the Ventura River "near the beach, on the shore of which there is a large town of pagans."[190] The founding of a mission to close the gap between San Luís Obispo and San Gabriel had long been delayed, and when it finally occurred, Serra commented: "The saying which was connected with the canonization of [Saint Bonaventure] may be applied to his mission: The longer it took, the more solemnly did we celebrate."[191] The present mission may be a bit farther from the shore than in Serra's day, a point that remains in contention. Serra visited three times. (211 Main Street, Ventura)

114. *San Buenaventura*, selected by Inspector General José de Gálvez as namesake for Mission San Buenaventura. The painting was commissioned much earlier than the mission's founding, since it was anticipated as mission number three, rather than nine. It was one of three rolled-up canvases Serra unexpectedly found in Monterey aboard the supply ship *San Antonio* in 1770. *San Buenaventura* and *San Diego*, the two surviving works, match in size, composition and artist. Saint Bonaventure (1221-1274, Italian Franciscan cardinal priest) wears a gray San Fernando College habit under his rochet, red cardinal's mantle and halo. He holds a church, symbolic of his title as *Doctor Seraphicus* (Seraphic Doctor) of the Church, and a quill in reference to his numerous theological and philosophical treatises. A crucifix stands on the table, reminder of his great devotion to Jesus. The painting is signed *"Josephus de Paez fecit, en México"* (José de Paez executed this, in Mexico). 32" x 41." (Mission San Buenaventura Museum, Ventura)

115. Santa Bárbara Royal Presidio Chapel, established by Serra as California's fourth and last military installation under Spain on 21 April 1782. He did not live to see the present structure, a 1985 replica of the 1797 chapel. Santa Bárbara, named after third-century Roman martyr Saint Barbara, was founded on "the edge of a grove of oaks apart from the beach and the Indian village, not very far from the lagoon."[192] Serra sang a Low Mass ending with the *Alabado* (a traditional Spanish hymn, from *alabar*, to praise) rather than a High Mass with *Te Deum* because he was the only priest present. He presumed he was founding Presidio-Mission Santa Bárbara, but the mission aspect of the enterprise was delayed until after his death and moved to a different site. He visited three times. (As for the final *presidio* not yet mentioned at San Francisco, Serra visited once in October 1777. As for San José and Los Angeles, the two *pueblos* founded by civil authorities during his presidency, he only visited Los Angeles, once in March 1782). (123 Cañon Perdido, Santa Barbara)

Post-Mortem

Wearing gray habit, cowl and cord, Junípero was placed in a simple redwood coffin shortly after his death on 28 August 1784. A violet silk stole was arranged around his neck and a small bronze reliquary cross in his clasped hands. Indian mourners laid wreaths of wildflowers at his bier, touched rosaries and medals to the body and began snipping small pieces of habit and hair as *recuerdos* (mementos) of their departed *padre*. Francisco Palóu admonished against such "pious theft" and counseled that relics were to be associated only with canonized saints.

On 29 August, all Monterey Presidio soldiers and 600 Mission Carmel Indians attended a morning Requiem High Mass, followed by burial in the mission church at four in the afternoon. After the central vault on the Gospel side of the sanctuary floor was blessed and incensed, final prayers were said and the coffin was lowered into the ground. Farewell tokens of earth were thrown in and as the final response was sung, "the tears, sighs and cries of those assisting drowned out the voices of the chanters."[193]

Immediately following, Francisco was besieged with more requests for *recuerdos* from soldiers, sailors and Indians. Tunics, underclothing and handkerchiefs were cut into scapulars, and the royal surgeon commented: "With this little cloth I expect to effect more cures than with my books and pharmacy."[194] He subsequently placed it on the head of a sailor with headaches and insomnia, who fell into a deep sleep and awakened the next morning without pain.

Francisco offered Junípero's hairshirt to Father Antonio Paterna, visiting from Mission San Luís Obispo. Gravely ill and contemplating the Last Sacraments, he put on the garment "and in a short time got well, . . . [and] was already saying Mass."[195] Before returning to Mission San Francisco, Francisco penned Junípero's four-page obituary in Mission Carmel's *Libro de Difuntos* on 5 September, wherein he noted he had been "very learned, . . . highly respected, . . . [and] always setting an example for everyone, . . . with his zeal and wisdom."[196]

News of Junípero's death spread quickly, and in the official correspondence to Majorca he was described as

> a happy soul [who] went directly to Heaven to enjoy the reward for thirty-four years of great and continuous labors, undergone for our beloved Jesus, whom he ever kept in mind, suffering them in an inexplicable manner for our redemption. So great was his charity which he always manifested toward those poor Indians that not only the ordinary people, but likewise persons of higher condition were struck with admiration. All men said openly that the man was a saint and that his actions were those of an apostle. This has been the opinion concerning him ever since he arrived in this kingdom. This opinion has been constant and without interruption.[197]

Junípero did not want fame and openly disdained all honors and tributes while alive. However, settlers and native people alike kept his "saintly" memory alive and his "fame of sanctity" continued to grow. Americans continued the tradition and celebrated the centennial of his death with a Mass and elaborate ceremony at his grave on 28 August 1884. "Fully 2,000" attended, including California Governor George Stoneman, General Mariano Guadalupe Vallejo, four bishops and "some old, old Indian[s], wrinkled like pippins, . . . in their brightest colored garments."[198] Governor Stoneman appealed to "the people of California," asking that Mission Carmel, "one of the first fruits of civilization in our beloved state, be restored in a manner worthy of the good pioneer priest Junípero Serra."[199] Through the efforts of many, the abandoned mission and gravesite would eventually be fully restored and privately maintained.

In 1891, the first public Serra monument in the world was erected only yards from where Junípero founded Presidio-Mission San Carlos Borromeo, the present city of Monterey. In 1913, the bicentennial of his birth was celebrated throughout California and Governor Hiram Johnson declared: "To the memory of Junípero Serra, California owes an everlasting tribute. He brought civilization to our land, and in deed and character he deserves a foremost place in the history of our state."[200] In 1931, he was selected as one of two citizens to represent the state in the U.S. Capitol's Statuary Hall, where he stands holding a cross and Mission Carmel replica. Due to its historical significance as Junípero's burial place, Mission Carmel Church was elevated to the rank of "minor basilica" by the Vatican in 1961, and streams of visitors have paid their respects at his grave, including His Holiness Pope John Paul II, several U.S. presidents and royalty. Coins, stamps, medals, books, plays, poems and various other tributes continue to be issued to this day.

On 28 August 1934, the Canonization Cause of Junípero Serra was formally introduced to the Vatican's Congregation for the Causes of Saints, a thirty-two member body of cardinals and archbishops appointed to consider such matters. History accounts for the delay. Spanish California passed to Mexico in 1821 and to the United States in 1846, so everything Spanish was for a time forgotten. Also, the Franciscan Province of Santa Barbara, which initiated the Cause, was not established until 1915, so prior to that Franciscan issues were handled by the Missouri Province, which had no abiding interest in the missions or Junípero.

The Cause proceeded under the direction of Most Reverend Philip Scher, D.D., Bishop of Monterey-Fresno; Reverend Eric O'Brien, O.F.M., Vice-Postulator (American administrator of the Cause and liaison with the Vatican); and a Diocesan Historical Commission composed of Herbert Bolton, Ph.D., Professor Emeritus of History, University of California, Berkeley; Reverend Maynard Geiger, O.F.M., Ph.D., Mission Santa Barbara Archivist and Historian of the Franciscan Province of Santa Barbara; and Right Reverend Monsignor James Culleton, D.D., J.C.D., Chancellor-Secretary of the Diocese of Monterey-Fresno.

From 30 August 1943 to 7 July 1949, the Informative Process of the Cause canonically (following Catholic Church law) exhumed Junípero's body for proof of identification; interviewed scores of descendants of people who knew him in a tribunal "court-of-law" format throughout California; and gathered more than 8,000 pages of documents about him from 125 libraries, archives and personal holdings in Spain, Mexico and California. Junípero's personal letters, philosophy and theology lectures, sermons, diary and official reports were combined with all other pertinent contemporary documents, ecclesiastical court records and modern literature, and then forwarded to the Vatican. There, the Congregation began the meticulous process of studying the life of Servant of God Junípero (a title given to the candidate during the process of inquiry) to search for doctrinal purity and to determine if *fama sanctitatis* (holiness) through "heroic virtue" existed (having lived a life of extraordinary Faith, Hope, Charity, Prudence, Justice, Temperance and Fortitude).

By 1981, the Serra Cause documents were condensed into a 650-page *Positio Super Vita et Virtutibus* (*Position on the Life and Virtues*), an official biography also known as a "Summarium." The highly technical dissertation, similar to a legal brief, presented Junípero as a formal candidate for sainthood to the Congregation, of whom its eleven historical consultants were required to answer the following questions: (1) Do the documents which have been collected, critically examined, and scientifically edited for the purpose of describing the life and activity of Servant of God Junípero Serra deserve historical acceptance and are sufficient and suitable? (2) Is the genuine reputation of the sanctity of the Servant of God proved by these same documents? (3) Is it possible for the theological consultors to use these same documents to find certain proofs to establish the fact that the Servant of God practiced virtues?

On 17 February 1982, the members voted affirmatively on all points and the Ordinary or historical process of Junípero's Cause was concluded, and the Apostolic or theological process initiated. His name was then submitted to Pope John Paul II with the petition that he declare Junípero "Venerable," that is, having lived a life of "heroic virtue," and thereby "worthy of veneration." This would be the last major step before beatification and canonization.

On 28 August 1984, all of California's bishops gathered at Junípero's Mission Carmel grave for a Mass commemorating the bicentennial of his death. His Eminence Timothy Cardinal Manning, Archbishop of Los Angeles, said in his homily:

> The seed must die in order to bear fruit. . . . This holy seed, which is the mortal remains of Junípero Serra . . . lies buried beneath us, and out of that burial has come the flowering of the Church in California. And so we, [the bishops] representing all the dioceses of California, assemble here today to recognize this particular gift that God has given to this fair land, [and] to make an affirmation of the sanctity of this holy friar, [and] to petition our Heavenly Father that the Cause of his elevation to the ranks of the beatified or the canonized may be accelerated by our presence, and certainly that this event would be brought to the notice of the Sacred Congregation.[201]

For the bicentennial, the U.S. Congress and California Legislature declared 28 August a "national day of recognition of Junípero Serra," and Junípero was eulogized in the House of Representatives by Hon. Leon Panetta, U.S. Representative, Sixteenth District. He said in part:

> Junípero Serra is to the Pacific Coast what the Pilgrims are to New England, a founding father. . . . He represents the beginning of American history from their western perspective, . . . [and] a striking contrast to the other explorers of our continent, driven not out of personal adventure or interest but from a spiritual mission. Father Serra sought not to conquer an unknown region but to cultivate its land and educate its people. . . . [Let us now] recognize his central role in the Spanish settlement of America and the national importance of his efforts.[202]

On 12 February 1985, the eight theological consultors of the Congregation unanimously agreed that Junípero practiced Christian virtue to a heroic degree. The Cardinal members of the Congregation ratified the findings on 2 April, and on 9 May 1985, Pope John Paul II declared Junípero "Venerable." This was a purely human affirmation. To proceed to the next step of beatification as a "local saint" with limited public veneration and the title "Blessed" (from the Latin *beatus*, "happy"), a search had to be made for unequivocal confirmation of God's approval of Junípero and his life, that is, a spontaneous, *bona fide* miracle performed through Junípero's intercession before God, "beyond all the laws of nature and medical art."[203]

After beatification, one more miracle would be required, taking place *after* the beatification, to proceed to the final stage of canonization and the title "Saint" (from the Latin *sanctus*, "holy"). At that point, the Pope would infallibly declare that Junípero practiced Christian virtue to a heroic degree, is in glory with God in Heaven and thereby worthy of public honor by the universal Catholic Church, and of imitation by all the faithful. After canonization, Saint Junípero would be accorded the following: the faithful can pray to him for intercession before God; Masses can be offered in his name with a special liturgy; a "feast day" can be designated on the Church's liturgical calendar; and his "relics," that is, small parts of his body or possessions can be distributed for public and private veneration.

The Congregation investigated several reports for the first miracle, including one involving Sister Mary Boniface Dyrda, O.S.F., a Franciscan Sister of Our Lady of Perpetual Help in St. Louis, Missouri. In 1960, the forty-four-year-old nun was diagnosed with incurable systemic lupus erythematosus, an inflammatory connective tissue disorder that brought her near death. In her words:

> My condition grew worse [after several months of tests and operations]. . . . My weight fell from 143 to 86 pounds, . . . and my doctor held out no hope of recovery. . . . I, as well as others had prayed and made novenas to obtain the intercession of [several saints], but none helped me as far as my sickness was concerned. Apparently they were waiting to give Father Junípero Serra a chance. For, when I was taken to De Paul Hospital to die, our chaplain suggested that [the other sisters and I] make a novena in honor of Father Serra. . . . [We did, and then] there was quite a sudden change on Good Friday 15 April 1960. . . . I sat up in bed, asked for an apple, and wanted to take a walk. My actions so startled the nurses that they called it a miracle and ran for the doctor. . . . I began to eat well, . . . experienced a steady improvement, and after another week I was dismissed. . . . Thanks be to God and to Father Serra![204]

On 8 July 1987, after two years of intensive scrutiny by the five physicians of the Medical Subcommittee of the Congregation, Sister Mary Boniface's cure was deemed scientifically unexplainable.

On 17 September 1987, Pope John Paul II visited Venerable Junípero's Mission Carmel grave as part of his second pastoral visit to the United States, where he paused to bless it, lay a wreath and pray. In his Mission Carmel Basilica address in English, he said in part:

> I come today as a pilgrim to this Mission of San Carlos, which so powerfully evokes the heroic spirit and heroic deeds of Fray Junípero Serra and which enshrines his mortal remains. This serene and beautiful place is truly the historical and spiritual heart of California. All the missions bear witness to the challenges and heroism of an earlier time, but not a time forgotten or without significance for

the California of today and the Church of today. . . . Very often at crucial moments in human affairs God raises up men and women whom he trusts into roles of decisive importance for the future development of both society and Church. . . . We rejoice all the more when their achievement is coupled with a holiness that can truly be called heroic. So it is with Junípero Serra, who in the providence of God was destined to be the Apostle of California and to have a permanent influence over the spiritual patrimony of this land and its people. . . . Father Serra was a man convinced of the Church's mission, conferred upon her by Christ, to evangelize the world, to "make disciples of all nations." . . . We too are called to be evangelizers, to share actively in the Church's mission of making disciples of all people. The way in which we fulfill that mission will be different from theirs. But their lives speak to us still because of their sure faith that the Gospel is true and because of their passionate belief in the value of bringing that saving truth to others at great personal cost. . . . "In him who is the source of my strength I have strength for everything" (Philippians 4:13). These words of the great missionary, Saint Paul, remind us that our strength is not our own. Even in the martyrs and saints, as the liturgy reminds us, it is "(God's) power shining through our human weakness" (Preface of Martyrs). It is the strength that inspired Father Serra's motto: "Always go forward, never back." It is the strength that one senses in this place of prayer so filled with his presence. It is this strength that can make each one of us, brothers and sisters, missionaries of Jesus Christ, witnesses of his message, doers of his word.[205]

On 13 November 1987, Venerable Junípero's remains were once again exhumed from his grave for the purpose of "canonically [re]identifying the remains . . . and, looking forward to his approaching beatification, for the purpose of recovering small [relic] parts separated from the body to satisfy the devotion of the faithful."[206]

On 1 December 1987, the full ten-member plenary of the Congregation voted that Sister Mary Boniface's cure was the result of Venerable Junípero's intercession before God, that is, miraculous. On 11 December, Pope John Paul II confirmed all previous findings and approved Venerable Junípero's beatification, which took place on Sunday 25 September 1988 during an elaborate ceremony and Papal Mass on the steps of Saint Peter's Basilica in Vatican City. In his Italian homily, the Holy Father said in part:

In Fray Junípero Serra . . . we find a shining example of Christian virtue and the missionary spirit. His great good was to bring the Gospel to the native peoples of America so that they too might be "consecrated in the truth." For many years, he devoted himself to this task in Mexico, in the Sierra Gorda and in California. He sowed the seeds of Christian faith amid the momentous changes wrought by the arrival of European settlers in the New World. It was a field of missionary endeavor that would require patience, perseverance and humility, as well as vision and courage. Relying on the divine power of the message he proclaimed, Father Serra led the native peoples to Christ. . . . In fulfilling this ministry, [he] showed himself to be a true son of Saint Francis. . . . [You] are Blessed because you see

God. Be near to us, to lead us along the way of truth to the same beatific vision.[207]

On 28 August 1989, the first official Mass was offered in Blessed Junípero's honor. Most Reverend Thaddeus Shubsda, D.D., Bishop of Monterey in California, was principal celebrant and homilist at Mission Carmel Basilica. He said Blessed Junípero "not only called us to share in the Good News, but told us not to count the cost in following in the example of the suffering of Christ, a suffering that leads to the glory that is the Resurrection."[208] He also initiated the Confraternity of Blessed Junípero Serra in the Diocese of Monterey, to promote the process of Blessed Junípero's canonization and to increase spiritual development among its members through emulation of his virtues.

On 9 December 1989, the Vatican's Congregation for Divine Worship and the Discipline of the Sacraments confirmed the decision of the United States Conference of Catholic Bishops to transfer the date of the "optional memorial" feast day of Blessed Junípero in the Church's liturgical calendar. 1 July was chosen to coincide with his first entry into California on 1 July 1769, as opposed to 28 August, his *die natalis* ("birthday" into Heaven, the traditional feast day), which is already the "obligatory memorial" of Saint Augustine of Hippo. Also, the Congregation announced that new churches in Quartz Hill and Camarillo, California would be the first in the world named after Blessed Junípero.

On 1 July 1990, Blessed Junípero's first official "feast day" Mass was celebrated at Mission Carmel Basilica by Bishop Shubsda. The liturgy ended with the following prayer for Blessed Junípero's canonization:

> Eternal God, moved by the promptings of Your divine grace, Blessed Junípero Serra, a priest of the Order of Friars Minor, went "ever forward" from his native Majorca to Mexico and to California to extend the kingdom of Christ to the shores of the sunset sea. Because he planted the seeds of the true faith, watered them with his sweat and tears, and lived a life of penance petitioning You to give the people of his western rim of Christianity growth in their faith, we humbly beseech You to grant that he be found worthy to have his name entered on the list of those whom the Church calls saints. We ask this, O God, in the name of Your divine Son, Jesus. Amen.[209]

Rº del Aº Pº Predº Frº Junipero Serra, Natl de la Villa de Petra en él Rno de Mallórca. Tomó el Habito en aquella Observlº Provª Haviendo profesado, y concluido sus estudios; leyo por tres años el Curso de ... el que finalizado obtuvo la Borla y Cathedra de Prima de Theologia del S.D. Escoto en aquella Rál, y Pontificia Universidad la que despues de algunos años renuncio, para venir en Mision á este Coleño de Sn Fernando de México. llegó dia 2. de Abril del añº de 1750 en q. por 3.ª ... fue Maestro de Novicios. por otros 3. Discreto. Salio varias vezes á misionar entre Infieles, donde manifestó su singular talento, y ardiente Caridad, de su ardiente pecho. Estube en calidad de Prº en las Misiones de Sierra Gorda, donde con Zelo infatigable trabajó en la reduccion de aquellos Indios. De alli paso á las Misiones de la vieja California por Presidente de todas ellas; de aqui entro al descubrimiento de las tierras de Monte ... fundó 9 Misiones, y confirmó é ellas mas de 5300 Indios, y despues de 14 añºs de Presidencia en estas, y muchos trabajos, y añºs verdaderamte Apostolicos, adornada su Alma de virtudes, se dispuso para la Exercicio, é prevenion, q. tubo sudado ... ansito. pues vno ú dos dias antes mundo se levanta un ... para enterrar su Cuerpo ... llamo á su Padre Confesor para la ultima Confeson; fue á la Iglesia á recivir el ... Viatico, cantando al mismo tiempo de recivirle con la mayor inclelia la Extrema del ... ... viam ecclesiæ sacramentum. buelto á su Celda, y sentado en vna silla, recivio con la mayor Devocion el Sacramento de la Extremauncion, rezando conlos Psalmos y circunstantes los Psalmos penitenciales; habiludos despues con alguna turbacion ... ... pue se le encomendara su Alma á Dios, á que respondio honrado de rodillas, finalizada esta funcion, exclamó con alegria y se galar jubilo; Gracias á Dios ya no hay miedo; descansare un rato, y recostandose sobre las tablas ... entregó el A ... su Criador, dia 28. de Agosto del año de 1784.

116. *Serra's Viaticum* (left). What did Serra look like? No one knows for sure. Here follows a description (plates 116 through 120) of how he *may* have looked, from the group of five historical portraits that are the source of all modern depictions. Shortly after Serra's death, Francisco Palóu commissioned his portrait wearing a "stole [over a gray habit, and holding a Communion veil to catch any particles that might fall from the Host], and kneeling before the altar of Our Lady [of Bethlehem, at Mission Carmel the day before he died], with the Child in her arms, and a priest vested with the cope before the altar, with a small host for giving him the Viaticum, and coming from the lips of the dead father in verse *Tantum ergo*, with many Indians and leather-jackets [soldiers] with their candles in their hands."[210] The seven-foot-square oil on canvas, painted in Mexico City by Mariano Guerrero in 1785, was kept at San Fernando College until at least 1853. Turning up as Mexican government property in 1904, the painting is now in the collection of the National History Museum, Chapultepec Palace, Mexico City. Nothing is known about the artist, although he may have been a Franciscan. There is no proof he knew Serra, worked from a more detailed description than Palóu's 1784 letter request from California, or waited for Palóu's 1785 return to Mexico City to paint Serra's face. Therefore, the veracity of his features remain open to question, especially considering that the painting was intended more as memorial to Serra than as historical record. The painting is signed "*Mariannus Guerrero fecit a. v 1785*" (Mariano Guerrero executed this in the year 1785). The Spanish legend translates: "True portrait of the Apostolic Father Preacher Fray Junípero Serra, native of the town of Petra, in the kingdom of Majorca. He took the habit of that Observant Province. After taking vows and finishing his studies, he lectured on the Arts for three years. At the end of this period, he received his [doctoral] tassel, and the Duns Scotus Chair *de prima* of Sacred Theology, in that Royal and Pontifical University. After several years, he resigned the post to come to this Apostolic College of San Fernando of Mexico, where he arrived on 2 April 1750 [*sic*] [1 January 1750]. He was a teacher of novices for three years, and then, an adviser to the superior for three years. He left several times to do missionary work among the faithful, where he showed extraordinary talent and ardent charity of his fervent heart. He was *presidente* of the missions of Sierra Gorda, where he worked with untiring zeal to convert those Indians. From there, he went to the missions of Old California to serve as *presidente*. From there, he initiated the discovery of the lands of Monterey, where he founded nine missions, and where he confirmed more than 5,300 in those missions. After fourteen [*sic*] [fifteen] years as *presidente* of the missions, and so much exhausting work, which was truly apostolic, his soul adorned with virtues, he prepared himself for eternity with certain knowledge of his death, for several days earlier he requested a coffin to be made to bury his body. He called his Father confessor [Palóu] for his last Confession, went to the church to receive the Holy Viaticum, and while receiving it, he very melodiously sang the verse of the hymn *Tantum ergo, Sacramentum*. Back in his cell, and seated on a chair, he received the Sacrament of Extreme Unction with much devotion. With the attending priests, he prayed the penitential psalms. Later, feeling a disturbance of his spirit, he asked on his knees for them to commend his soul to God. Once the act was finished, he exclaimed with happiness and jubilation: "Thank God, now there is no fear; I will rest for a while," and lying down on [his bed] of boards, he surrendered his soul to the Creator on 28 August 1784."

V. R. DEL V. P. F. JUNIPERO SERRA

hijo de la S.ta Prov.a de N.P.S. Fran.co de la Isla de Mallorca D.r y Ex.o de Th.a Cmis.o del S.to Of.o J.r del Ap.co Col.o de S. Fern.o de Mex.co Fund.r y Presid.te de las Miss.es de la Calif.a Septentr.l = Mu.ro con gr.de Fama de Sant.d en la Miss.n de S. Carlos del Pu.o del N. Monte Rey á 28. de Ag.to de la de edad de 70. a.s 9m.s 4 d.s hab.o gastado la mit.d de su vida en el exercc.o de Mission.o Apost.co

117. Palóu Woodcut Serra Portrait, a frontispiece engraving from Francisco Palóu's 1787 biography of Serra. Serra is shown in Franciscan habit, holding a crucifix, and a stone in his right hand representing a life of penance undertaken for his sins and the sins of others. Tears signify pathos for the souls he left unredeemed and the birds above him those he helped redeem. He is surrounded by his European and Indian congregation, and at his feet: a skull (mortality); lighted candle (immortality); chain (self-mortification); scallop shell (attribute of Saint Augustine of Hippo, on whose feast day Serra died, and of Saint James the Greater, patron of Serra's Spanish homeland); chalice with snake (attribute of Saint John the Evangelist, in reference to his miraculous escape from death by poisoning, as did Serra in the Mexican Sierra Gorda). No known record corroborates the authenticity of Serra's features. The engraving, featured in Palóu's *Relación Histórica de la Vida y Apostólicas Tareas del Venerable Padre Fray Junípero Serra* (*Historical Account of the Life and Apostolic Labors of the Venerable Father Fray Junípero Serra*) was first published in Mexico City in 1787. Authored by Serra's longtime friend and fellow Majorcan, this was the first book written in California. Palóu (1723-1789) felt compelled to write about Serra, not just from a hagiographical point of view, but so that "he shall be forever in the memory of all."[211] A few hundred copies were printed and distributed in Mexico, California, Majorca and even the royal palace in Madrid. The first English translation appeared in 1884 and today this important primary source of information provides the "basic text employed by writers in producing the books, articles, brochures, pageants and orations about Serra that in almost endless succession have appeared down to our day."[212] The Spanish legend translates: "True portrait of the Venerable Father Fray Junípero Serra, son of the holy province of Our Seraphic Saint Francis on the Island of Majorca; Doctor and Ex-Professor of Theology, Commissary of the Holy Office, Missionary of the Apostolic College of San Fernando of Mexico, Founder and President of the Missions of Upper California. He died with great fame of holiness on 28 August 1784 at the age of 70 years, 9 months, 4 days, having spent half of his life as an apostolic missionary."

118. San Fernando Serra Portrait, a black-and-white engraving that first appeared in an article about Serra's life by M. Roa Barcena in *La Cruz* magazine, Mexico City, volume III, number 10, 9 October 1856, page 303. Presumed to have been copied from an older, lost original painting, Serra sits in an eighteenth-century Mexican-style armchair, wearing a Franciscan habit. The assumption is that he posed for a portrait while staying at San Fernando College during his last visit to Mexico City in 1773, although there is no record of this.

119. Querétaro Serra Portrait (see front cover), the most commonly reproduced Serra image. He is incorrectly portrayed with greenish-gray eyes (his were dark) and a ruddy complexion (his was olive *moreno*). However, he correctly wears a gray habit and the large crucifix he brought from Majorca, and the portrait's overall effect at least imparts a more lifelike countenance than the preceding two. The Spanish legend at the painting's base (not shown on the cover) translates: "Portrait of the Reverend Father Junípero Serra, Apostle of Upper California, copied from the original which is kept in his convent of Santa Cruz in Querétaro. Painted by Father José Mosqueda." Mosqueda (1870-1954) made two identical 26" by 20" oil on canvas copies before the original disappeared during the 1910-17 Mexican Revolution, one of which is displayed in Mission Santa Bárbara's Archive-Library. The other is presumed lost. Nothing more is known about the original, although it may have been painted when Serra visited Mexico City in 1773.

120. Zacatecas Serra Portrait (right). This 12-1/2" by 9-1/2" tempera-on-paper image, painted on mid-to-late nineteenth-century paper in light, delicate brush strokes indicative of copying, was discovered in a Zacatecas, Mexico second-hand store in 1954 by Mission Carmel Curator Harry Downie. The sketch, presumed from an older, lost original painting, is preserved in Mission Carmel Archives. The Spanish legend, with several technical errors, translates: "Fray Junípero Serra Founder of the holy missions of San Diego, San Carlos Borromeo de Monterey, San Gabriel, San Luís Obispo, San Francisco de Asís, and San Juan Capistrano of Upper California. Sketch by Pedro Pablo Mguez. Convento of the [Holy] Cross. Province of the Holy Gospel. Queréta[ro]." Nothing more is known about the original, the copy or the artist. With downcast eyes under a Majorcan light blue, hooded cowl, the Zacatecas physiognomy matches the sick, weary Serra of 1773, "twice at the gates of death" en route to Mexico City, more than the other robust, embonpoint renderings. Could this be the "true" Serra likeness? It conforms more than the others to the Vatican's 1943 canonical exhumation report, in which experts who examined Serra's skull concluded: "[We] visualize . . . a well-shaped head, long but not markedly narrow. . . . The nose is straight and runs upward to join the moderately high forehead. . . . The cheeks are somewhat sunken thus accentuating the well-formed cheekbones while the firm, somewhat pointed chin must have been a notable feature. [In contrast, the other portraits project greater breadth of head and face]."[213] One theory is that the Palóu Woodcut, San Fernando and Querétaro portraits share a common root in *Serra's Viaticum*. The Woodcut was executed two years after the *Viaticum*, and the San Fernando and Querétaro portraits could be nineteenth-century renditions excerpted from the *Viaticum* rather than originals painted when Serra visited Mexico City for the last time, and then copied later. With the veracity of the keystone *Viaticum* features already in doubt, the integrity of the subsequent three is thereby challenged as well. Reverend Maynard Geiger, O.F.M., Ph.D., Serra historian for nearly fifty years, offered the only tenable conclusion concerning all five portraits: "Because of the tenuous evidence . . . we cannot point to any of the extant Serra paintings or prints and say this one to the exclusion of all others represents Serra as he really was. . . . The only answer an honest historian can give [is] . . . I do not know."[214]

Fray Junípero Serra Fundador de las Santas Misiones
de S. Diego, S. Carlos Boromeo de Monterrey, S. Gabriel, S. Luis Ob.
S. Fco de Asis y San Juan Capistrano de Alta California

Boceto de Pedro Pablo Miguez Conto de la Cruz
Prov. del St. En Orusela

LV.º Pᵉ Mº FR. JUNIPERO SERRA, FUNDADOR DE LAS MISIO-
ES DE LA CALIFORNIA SEPTENTᴸ NACIÓ EN PÉTRA EN 24 NOVᵉ
E 1713 Y MURIÓ EN LA MISION DE Sᴺ CARLOS EN 28 AGOSTO DE 178

121. Palma Serra Portrait, a fanciful depiction of Serra at the moment he expressed "great fear"
shortly before dying. Francisco Palóu reads the "Commendation for a Departing Soul" and holds
an aspergill to sprinkle Serra's cell with holy water. Note the incongruous bamboo chair and Indian
in full feather headdress peering over Palóu's shoulder. Commissioned by the city of Palma,
Majorca in 1790, and painted by Fray Andrés Caymari, the unsigned oil on canvas hangs in the
Hall of Famous Personages, Palma City Hall, Palma. The Spanish legend translates: "Portrait of
the Venerable Father Missionary Fray Junípero Serra, Founder of the Missions of Upper California.
Born in Petra on 24 November 1713, and died at the Mission of San Carlos on 28 August 1784."

122. Mission Carmel, September 1787. Executed by French La Pérouse Expedition artist Gaspard Duché de Vancy, this earliest-known sketch of Mission Carmel shows the reception of the first "foreign" visitor to a California mission. Fermín de Lasuén, second *padre-presidente* of the missions, stands in the doorway of Mission Carmel's fifth church, the Serra Adobe within which Serra was interred at the foot of the sanctuary on 29 August 1784. To the left of the church, Serra's 1771 founding cross stands in the courtyard. To the right, Indian bellringers announce La Pérouse's arrival.

123. Mission Carmel, November 1794. Executed by English Vancouver Expedition artist John Sykes, the sketch shows the graves of Serra and Juan Crespí marked by a small, stout cross in the courtyard. The Serra Adobe Church was dismantled in 1793 to make way for the present sandstone church, completed in 1797. Its sacristy, with thatched roof to the right of the cross, was built first to train the Indian craftsmen. When the nave was built, the burial vaults were left untouched and incorporated into a new, larger sanctuary. The provisional sixth church, used from February 1793 to September 1797, is on the far left next to the bells.

124. Mission Carmel, circa 1877. After issuance of Mexico's *Reglamento Provisional* (*Provisional Regulation*) of 1834, a harsh "secularization" decree authorizing termination of the mission system and civil confiscation of all mission property, the California mission chain slowly fell into ruin. Mission Carmel's last resident priest left in 1845 and the church's heavy stone, wood and tile roof began to collapse in winter 1852. All movable furnishings were taken to Monterey's Royal Presidio Chapel for safekeeping, and kept there until the restoration of 1930-50. On the far left, at the northeast corner of the north wing of the quadrangle, stood Serra's cell.

125. Mission Carmel interior, circa 1870. The cross on the left side of the sanctuary marks the approximate site of Serra's grave, which had been relocated under four feet of debris and opened on 10-12 March 1856 under the authorization of Most Reverend Joseph Alemany O.P., California's first archbishop. In 1861, a tourist commented on Mission Carmel's desolation: "Cattle had free access to all parts; . . . broken columns were strewn around where the altar was; . . . thousands of birds, apparently, lived in nooks of the old deserted walls of the ruins; and the number of ground squirrels burrowing in the old mounds . . . was incredible."[215]

126. 3 July 1882 public viewing of Serra's grave (which did not disturb the remains), showing Reverend Angelo Casanova, Pastor of Monterey's San Carlos Church, holding Mission Carmel's *Libro de Difuntos* to read Serra's obituary and confirm that he had been buried on the "Gospel side of the sanctuary"; Mission Carmel caretaker Christiano Machado sitting on the edge of Serra's vault; California National Guard "Legion of Saint Patrick" Cadets; California National Guard Third Regiment Band; and audience of nearly five hundred. Organized by Casanova, the viewing was a fundraiser for restoration of the mission in anticipation of the 1884 centennial of Serra's death. His efforts resulted in several interior restoration projects, including cleaning the interior and installing a new high-pitched roof on the church. He also sealed the sanctuary graves beneath a foot of concrete and stone when raising the level of the sanctuary floor in 1883, which protected them until their next opening in 1943.

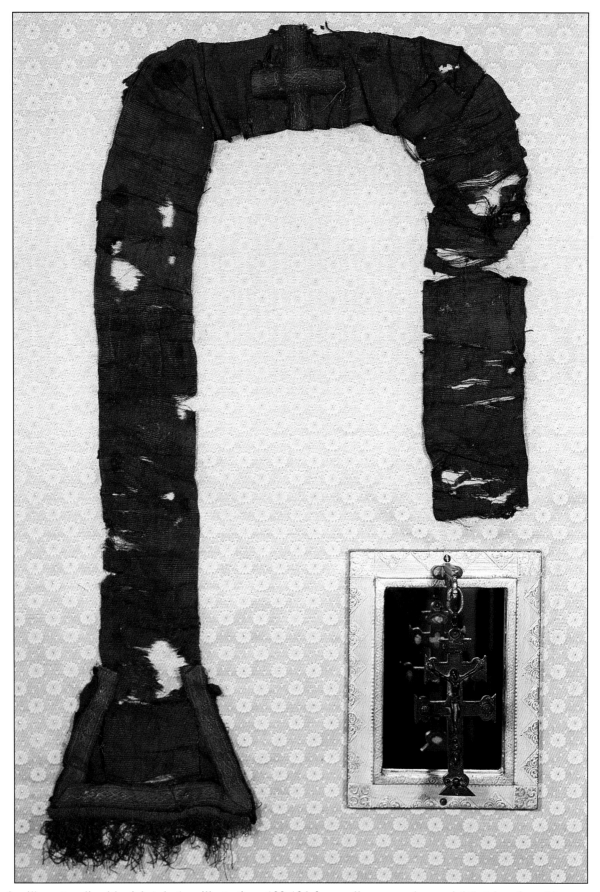

127. Serra's silk, cotton-lined burial stole (see illustrations 133-134 for small cross on lower right), taken from his grave by Father Casanova on 14 January 1882 (he privately entered Serra's grave before the 3 July 1882 public viewing to ensure that everything was intact). Approximately twenty percent is missing because Casanova cut it into very small pieces for distribution to those in attendance at the public viewing. The remainder was for a time divided in half and traveled to San Jose before being reunited and returned to Mission Carmel in 1938. Several methods were used to establish provenance, including comparison to a third small piece in a reliquary accompanied by a letter of authenticity signed by Casanova in 1882. The stole, worn by priests during the administration of the Sacraments, was placed around Serra's neck when he was buried. 56" x 3." (Mission Carmel Museum, Carmel)

128. Stanford Serra monument, circa 1891. Mrs. Jane Stanford, wife of former California governor and U.S. Senator Leland Stanford, donated $5,000 to erect a "unique and beautiful monument" to Serra on Monterey's Presidio Hill, approximately one hundred yards from the Vizcaíno-Serra landing cove. Sculpted from a sixteen-ton-block of California Crystal Lake granite, the 9'6" tall statue shows Serra stepping from a dinghy onto the shore. With facial features based on the San Fernando Serra Portrait, he wears a Franciscan habit, stole, and holds a book inscribed *Scripta Sacra* (*Sacred Scripture*). The large cross bears the 3 June 1770 date of Monterey's founding. With 5,000 in attendance, the first public Serra monument in the world was dedicated on 3 June 1891.

129. Petra Serra statue, circa 1915. Sculpted by Guillermo Galmes to commemorate the bicentennial of Serra's birth and placed in Petra's Plaza de Junípero Serra, the 6' statue on 11' base was dedicated before a crowd of 4,000 on 28 September 1913. When word reached California that donations had not paid all expenses, local schoolchildren collected pennies to pay for the statue, with enough left over to buy shoes for Petra's schoolchildren. With facial features based on the San Fernando Serra Portrait, Serra wears a Franciscan habit and holds a cross. The Franciscan and Petran coats of arms are sculpted on the pedestal's sides. A saw and anvil are on the back, referring to the etymology of Serra's name. Serra is the Catalonian form of the Castilian *sierra*, or saw. His mother's maiden name, Ferrer, translates to *herrero* in Castilian, or ironworker/blacksmith. On the front, in Mallorquín: "To the memory of the Venerable Father Junípero Serra, Franciscan, Apostle of the People of California. 1713-1784. His Country."

130. U.S. Statuary Hall Serra statue, circa 1931. Pursuant to an 1864 Act of Congress that created a national statuary hall and invited each state to donate two statues of citizens "illustrious for their renown because of distinguished civil or military service,"[216] the California State Legislature selected Serra and Thomas Starr King (1824-1864, Unitarian minister) as its representatives in 1927. Ettore Cadorin of Santa Barbara sculpted Serra in bronze for $12,500, with facial features based on the San Fernando Serra Portrait. He wears a Franciscan habit, holds a cross and a miniature replica of Mission Carmel (with Casanova's high-pitched 1882-1936 interim roof). The statue was accepted by Act of Congress into Statuary Hall, the U.S. Capitol Building, Washington, D.C. on 1 March 1931, at which time U.S. Secretary of the Interior Ray Wilbur, speaking on behalf of President Herbert Hoover, said: "Junípero Serra's name is reverent, his work enduring, his influence ever living."[217] The statue stands 8'9" on a 3'6" marble base, with the simple inscription: "Junípero Serra: California."

131. Serra's reinterment, 7 December 1943. As part of the Canonization Cause of Junípero Serra, an official exhumation was undertaken from 30 August to 7 December 1943. The remains of all three Mission Carmel sanctuary vaults (each measuring 7 feet long by 2 wide by 5 deep) were carefully removed, placed in secretly numbered boxes, and anonymously studied by two forensic pathologists and two physical anthropologists. Regarding the remains in the central vault, they concluded: "Tradition, historical fact, anthropology and archaeology combine overwhelmingly in establishing the identity of the cranium of the skeleton of Individual A as Father Serra, . . . a short-statured, small-boned, white male European . . . over sixty years at death. He was about five feet, two inches tall, . . . [a] small and wiry but well-proportioned man."[218] Since Serra's original redwood coffin was badly deteriorated, he received a new child-size, hermetically-sealed copper casket (his remains consisted of individual bones, not an articulated skeleton, so a full-size casket was not necessary). Serra was reinterred in his traditional burial place, the central vault, on the morning of 7 December. L-R: Reverend Constantine Badeson, Ecclesiastical Notary; Reverend Eric O'Brien, O.F.M., Serra Cause Vice-Postulator; Very Reverend John Durkin, V.F., Bishop's Delegate; Reverend Michael O'Connell, Mission Carmel Pastor; Harry Downie, Mission Carmel Curator; Reverend Lucien Arvin, J.C.D., Promoter of the Faith; Very Reverend Gregory Wooler, O.F.M., Provincial, Province of Santa Barbara, Order of Friars Minor.

132. Serra's remains, 7 December 1943.

133. Serra's bronze burial reliquary cross, discovered in his grave during the 1943 exhumation. The anthropologists concluded: "The reliquary was so clearly the product of a European craftsman . . . and the revelation of the object's connection with Blessed Raymond Llull . . . is evidence which no qualified archaeologist could hesitate to stress in the strongest terms as being critical to identifying the remains with which it was found as those of a priest, a native of Majorca."[219] Known as a *Cruz de Caravaca*, it is credited with winning battles and converting Moors after a supernatural vision in 1232 first revealed the distinctive double-crosspiece design to Gines Pérez, a priest imprisoned in the southern Spanish town of Caravaca during the Moorish occupation of Spain (711-1492). Serra's Caravaca cross is decorated with Christ Crucified and Our Lady of Sorrows at His feet. Above Christ's head, the letters INRI, acronym for the Latin *Iesus Nazarenus Rex Iudaeorum* (Jesus the Nazarean King of the Jews). Also, to the left of Christ on the lower crosspiece, the letters IHS, the first three letters of *IHSOUS*, the Greek spelling for the name Jesus. To the right, the letters AM, monogram for the Latin *Ave Maria* (Hail Mary). The skull and crossbones at the base is symbolic of Golgotha, and in reference to a medieval belief that the Cross was raised over Adam's grave, with Christ's sacrifice thereby serving to redeem mankind from Adam and Eve's Original Sin. 4-3/4" tall x 2-1/4" wide lower arm. (Mission Carmel Museum, Carmel)

134. Reverse side of Serra's open burial cross with nine unsealed cloth relics under glass. At least two pertain to Blessed Ramón Llull. The pieces of cloth were most likely touched to his grave in Palma's San Francisco Basilica, thereby becoming "relics." At some point they were brought to California and placed within the cross buried with Serra. The handwritten letters *San* (Saint in Spanish, or short for *Sanctus*, Saint in Latin) are clearly discernable over one relic, which could not pertain to *B. Raydi M* (*Beatus*, Blessed in Latin) Ramón Llull of Majorca. However, nothing more can be ascertained from the discolored, faded strips of paper.

135. Serra's Mission Carmel Basilica sanctuary grave and the remaining remnants of his original 1784 redwood coffin at the base. The Spanish epitaph translates: "Fray Junípero Serra: Apostle of California 1713-1784."

136. U.S. national Junípero Serra medal. By Act of Congress signed into law by President John Kennedy on 16 October 1963, a national medal was struck to commemorate the 250th anniversary of Serra's birth, which President Kennedy called a "reminder of our Spanish heritage whose values were exemplified in the piety, courage and vision of Father Serra."[220] The medal, designed by Chief U.S. Engraver Frank Gasparro, shows Serra as portrayed in the U.S. Capitol's Statuary Hall, and with replicas of the first *ten* missions on the reverse, since Serra *thought* he was founding Mission Santa Bárbara in 1782. The 1-5/16" diameter medal was minted in quantities of 5 fourteen-carat gold (proof); 25 platinum (proof); 10,000 silver (1,000 proof); and 82,000 bronze (1,000 proof) at the U.S. Mint in Philadelphia.

137. California Capitol State Park Serra monument, circa 1967. In 1963, California Governor Edmund Brown signed a bill providing up to $30,000 to erect and maintain a Serra statue on the grounds of California's State Capitol in Sacramento, provided a like amount could be raised privately. This was the first time the State of California had cooperated in a "joint venture" to honor a private individual with a statue. An 11'6" Serra, with facial features based on the San Fernando and Querétaro Portraits, is shown in a Franciscan habit and holding a cross. He stands on a bronze/marble California map depicting all twenty-one missions, and is surrounded by a walkway embedded with the façades of the nine missions founded during his presidency. The statue, dedicated on 8 April 1967, is located in a camellia grove at the intersection of two walkways on the east grounds, between 12th and 13th Streets.

138. Commencement of the Serra Bicentennial Concelebrated Mass at Mission Carmel Basilica, 28 August 1984. In the company of His Excellency Pio Laghi, S.T.D., J.C.D., Apostolic Pro-Nuncio in the United States; Very Reverend John Forman, O.F.M., Minister General, Order of Friars Minor; twenty-one U.S. and three Mexican bishops; and 125 priests, His Eminence Timothy Cardinal Manning, D.D., J.C.D., Archbishop of Los Angeles, was principal celebrant and homilist for a liturgical celebration honoring Serra on the bicentennial of his death. This marked the beginning of an international "Serra Year" of events and ceremonies, culminating in an outdoor Mass celebrated at Mission Carmel on 28 August 1985. President Ronald Reagan sent a telegram to the 1985 ceremony, which read in part: "I am pleased to send warm greetings to everybody participating in the solemn religious ceremonies concluding the bicentennial of the Venerable Father Serra's death. Father Serra is one of the heroes of our land. His tireless work for the Indians of California, despite distances and physical disabilities that would have daunted a lesser man, remains a shining page in our history."[221] Seated L-R: Most Reverend Thaddeus Shubsda, D.D., Bishop of Monterey in California; His Excellency Pio Laghi, S.T.D., J.C.D., Apostolic Pro-Nuncio in the United States; His Eminence Timothy Cardinal Manning, D.D., J.C.D., Archbishop of Los Angeles; Most Reverend John Quinn, D.D., Archbishop of San Francisco; Most Reverend Harry Clinch, D.D., Former Bishop of Monterey in California.

139. Junípero Serra U.S. commemorative airmail stamp. The long and complicated process of commemorating Serra on a U.S. postage stamp began in 1963 and finally by 1984, on the occasion of the bicentennial of his death, his name was accepted by the U.S. Postal Service. An airmail format was chosen to reflect his international appeal. The 1.56 by .99 inch stamp was designed by Richard Schlecht of Richmond, Virginia, and the model was created by Frank Waslick of the U.S. Bureau of Engraving and Printing. The design is based on Spain's forty *peseta* stamp issued in 1984, with Serra's likeness patterned after the Querétaro Serra Portrait in gray habit, and against a silhouette of the Californias and Mission San Gabriel's belltower. First-day-of-issue ceremonies took place in San Diego on 22 August 1985.

140. Pope John Paul II at Serra's grave, 1:30 p.m., 17 September 1987. After an outdoor Mass before a crowd of 50,000 at Monterey's Laguna Seca Raceway, the Holy Father visited Mission Carmel. At 1:25 he entered the basilica and greeted the invited audience of 450 dignitaries, multi-denominational church officials and parishioners as he walked up the aisle. At 1:30 he reached the altar where he knelt and prayed before the *reredos*. He then walked a few steps to Serra's grave and laid a wreath, drawing warm applause from the audience. He reflected for a moment at the grave (see back cover), blessed it, and then walked to the opposite side of the sanctuary to deliver a fifteen-minute address. Afterward, he recited the Our Father, blessed the audience, once again knelt to pray before the altar, stood for a few more moments at Serra's grave, and then proceeded down the aisle and into Our Lady of Bethlehem side chapel. Before exiting the chapel at 1:55, he paused to pray where Serra so often did, at the foot of Our Lady of Bethlehem, California's most historic statue.

141. Serra's 13 November 1987 canonical exhumation. Work began privately on the afternoon of 12 November to open the vault and remove the casket. It remained sealed until the following morning, when it was inspected and opened by Most Reverend Thaddeus Shubsda, Bishop of Monterey. The crucial moment involved "inspect[ing] the box [casket] diligently to verify the identity of the seals . . . to certainly verify that the remains are truly those of the Venerable Servant of God."[222] If the seal was violated, all 1943 findings could be invalidated, which would have stalled Serra's sainthood process. The copper wire

wound through holes in the fastening bolts of the inner glass lid was unbroken, and the lead rubric seal at the end was intact. One hundred-thirty-two pieces of bone were removed, placed on a table and cross-checked against a 1943 inventory. Once completed, small particles of bone were removed by the Vice-Postulator for transport to the Vatican, where they would be encapsulated in small relic cases for distribution to the faithful. The casket was then resealed and returned to the vault that afternoon. Seated L-R: Huu Van Nguyen, Mission Carmel Assistant Curator; Reverend Noel Moholy, O.F.M., S.T.D., Serra Cause Vice-Postulator; Miriam Downie, daughter of the late Mission Carmel Curator Sir Harry Downie, K.S.G.; Reverend Monsignor Francis Weber, Archivist, Archdiocese of Los Angeles; Reverend Joseph Conran, S.J., Associate Pastor, Mission Carmel Basilica. Standing L-R: Osman Hull, M.D., forensic pathologist, Monterey; David Huelsbeck, Ph.D., physical anthropologist, Santa Clara University; Most Reverend Thaddeus Shubsda, Bishop of Monterey; Virginia Klepich, Monterey Diocesan Ecclesiastical Notary; Joe Hinojos, official photographer for the 1943 exhumation; Reverend Thomas Keifer, Orat., Monterey Diocesan Promoter of Justice; Edward Soberanes, descendant of an early Spanish family associated with Mission Carmel; and Richard Menn, Monterey Diocesan Curator.

142. Serra's beatification in Saint Peter's Square, Vatican City, on Sunday 25 September 1988. The Papal Mass began at 9:30 a.m. when Pope John Paul II entered the square via the main door of Saint Peter's Basilica. Amidst the pealing of bells, choir music and an array of flowers decorating the altar on the steps of Saint Peter's, the Pope greeted the crowd of 30,000 pilgrims assembled for six concurrent beatifications. In attendance for Serra, the Bishops of Majorca, Spain; Querétaro, Mexico; and Monterey, California.

143. The solemn Rite of Beatification. Following the introductory prayers, the bishops from the dioceses of the candidates for beatification assembled before Pope John Paul II and extolled the life and virtues of each. Most Reverend Thaddeus Shubsda, Bishop of Monterey, stands fourth from left. Following the statements, the bishops formally petitioned the Pope to "inscribe in the number of the Blessed the Venerable Servants of God." Reading from an Apostolic Brief in Latin, the Pope declared: "On the basis of the decree of the Congregation for the Causes of Saints, by Our Apostolic Authority, [we] grant authority that the Venerable Servants of God . . . be called by the name of Blessed for the future and that their feast on their birthday into Heaven . . . be celebrated every year in the places and manner established by law. In the name of the Father, and of the Son, and of the Holy Spirit."[223] Following tradition, as soon as the Pope finished his declaration, portraits of the six newly-declared Blesseds were unfurled from the balconies of Saint Peter's Basilica and the *Gloria in Excelis Deo* (Glory to God in the Highest) was sung by the Vatican's Sistine Chapel Choir. The bishops individually greeted and kissed the Pope and then Mass proceeded, with the Pope delivering a homily focusing on the beatified and their roles in contemporary life. During the Offertory, gifts were presented to the Pope: in honor of Serra, six California eagle feathers in a leather pouch decorated with antique, red clay beads, presented by Andrew Galvan, a California Ohlone Indian; and a linen altar cloth embroidered with flowers, woven by the women of Petra and presented by Isabel Salom, director of the Serra Casa Solariega and Museum in Petra.

144. Painting of Serra unfurled from the balcony of Saint Peter's Basilica at the pronouncement of his beatification (see photograph 142, second balcony from the right). The 20' by 8' image, the first authorized for public veneration, was painted by Lorenzo Ghiglieri of Portland, Oregon. Serra, depicted against an ocher sunset and rocky California landscape, and with facial features based on a compilation of all five historic portraits (especially the Zacatecas Serra Portrait), wears a brown Franciscan habit and carries a hat and staff. An enlarged version of the Caravaca Cross he was interred with is around his neck, and in the lower right corner, a single California Wild Rose, a flower he often noted as the "Rose of Castile" on his California travels.

Notes

MAJORCA NARRATIVE

[1]Maynard Geiger, *Palóu's Life of Fray Junípero Serra* (Washington, D.C.: Academy of American Franciscan History, 1955), 3.

[2]Ibid.

[3]Ibid.

[4]Ibid., 4.

[5]Manuscript 882, Archivo del Estado, Majorca Public Library, Palma, p. 50.

[6]Geiger, *Palóu's Life of Fray Junípero Serra*, 5.

[7]Ibid.

[8]Maynard Geiger, *The Life and Times of Fray Junípero Serra, O.F.M.*, 2 vols. (Washington, D.C.: Academy of American Franciscan History, 1959), 1:21-22.

[9]Murray Bodo, *Juniper: Friend of Francis, Fool of God* (Cincinnati: St. Anthony Messenger Press, 1983), 1.

[10]Manuscript 76, Archivo del Estado, Majorca Public Library, Palma, p. 91.

[11]Geiger, *The Life and Times of Fray Junípero Serra, O.F.M.*, 1:27.

[12]Geiger, *Palóu's Life of Fray Junípero Serra*, 6.

[13]Ibid., 8.

[14]Ibid., 5.

[15]Ibid., 8.

[16]Ibid., 9.

[17]Ibid.

[18]Ibid., 11.

[19]Ibid., 12.

[20]Ibid.

[21]Geiger, *The Life and Times of Fray Junípero Serra, O.F.M.*, 1:58.

[22]Antonine Tibesar, ed., *Writings of Junípero Serra*, 4 vols. (Washington, D.C.: Academy of American Franciscan History, 1955-66), 1:3, 5, 9.

MAJORCA PHOTOGRAPHS

[23]Maynard Geiger, *Junípero Serra's Enduring Fame in Spain, Mexico, and California* (Santa Barbara: The Franciscan Fathers, 1960), 8.

[24]Ernest Ingold, *The House in Mallorca* (San Francisco: Paul Elder and Company, 1950), 11.

[25]Ibid., 23.

[26]Murray Bodo, *Juniper: Friend of Francis, Fool of God*, 20.

[27]Geiger, *The Life and Times of Fray Junípero Serra, O.F.M.*, 1:11.

[28]Mission San Carlos Borromeo *Libro de Bautismos*, Diocese of Monterey Chancery Archives, vol. 1, entry 750.

MEXICO NARRATIVE

[29]Tibesar, *Writings of Junípero Serra*, 1:17.

[30]Geiger, *Palóu's Life of Fray Junípero Serra*, 209.

[31]Ibid., 279-80.

[32]Ibid., 356.

[33]Ibid., 33.

[34]Ibid., 265.
[35]Ibid., 44.
[36]Ibid., 30.
[37]Ibid.
[38]Ibid., 29-31.
[39]Tibesar, *Writings of Junípero Serra*, 1:25.
[40]Geiger, *Palóu's Life of Fray Junípero Serra*, 46.
[41]Ibid., 47.
[42]Ibid., 19.
[43]Ibid., 46.
[44]Geiger, *The Life and Times of Fray Junípero Serra, O.F.M.*, 1:201.
[45]Geiger, *Palóu's Life of Fray Junípero Serra*, 63.
[46]Ibid., 62.
[47]Geiger, *Palóu's Life of Fray Junípero Serra*, 65.
[48]Tibesar, *Writings of Junípero Serra*, 1:63.
[49]Ibid., 1:65.
[50]Geiger, *Palóu's Life of Fray Junípero Serra*, 67.
[51]Ibid.
[52]Tibesar, *Writings of Junípero Serra*, 1:77.
[53]Ibid., 1:83.
[54]Ibid., 1:107.
[55]Ibid., 1:113.
[56]Ibid., 1:135.

MEXICO PHOTOGRAPHS

[57]Geiger, *Palóu's Life of Fray Junípero Serra*, 279.
[58]Ibid., 33.
[59]Herbert Bolton, *Historical Memoirs of New California* (Berkeley: University of California Press, 1926), 4:356-57.
[60]Ibid., 56.
[61]Ibid., 55.

CALIFORNIA NARRATIVE

[62]Tibesar, *Writings of Junípero Serra*, 1:121.
[63]Ibid.
[64]Ibid., 1:143.
[65]Ibid., 1:123.
[66]Ibid., 1:137.
[67]Geiger, *Palóu's Life of Fray Junípero Serra*, 75.
[68]Ibid., 78.
[69]Tibesar, *Writings of Junípero Serra*, 1:155.
[70]Ibid., 1:151.
[71]Ibid., 1:173, 269.
[72]Geiger, *Palóu's Life of Fray Junípero Serra*, 86.
[73]Tibesar, *Writings of Junípero Serra*, 1:139,153; and Geiger, *Palóu's Life of Fray Junípero Serra*, 278.
[74]Geiger, *Palóu's Life of Fray Junípero Serra*, 87.
[75]Ibid., 87-88.
[76]Tibesar, *Writings of Junípero Serra*, 1:169.

[77]Ibid., 1:168-69, 171.

[78]Ibid., 1:171.

[79]Ibid., 1:391.

[80]Ibid., 1:171, 4:259.

[81]Geiger, *Palóu's Life of Fray Junípero Serra*, 116.

[82]Tibesar, *Writings of Junípero Serra*, 1:255, 353.

[83]Ibid., 1:257, 351, 353.

[84]Ibid., 1:351.

[85]Geiger, *Palóu's Life of Fray Junípero Serra*, 132.

[86]Tibesar, *Writings of Junípero Serra*, 1:257.

[87]Ibid., 1:393.

[88]Geiger, *Palóu's Life of Fray Junípero Serra*, 415.

[89]Ibid., 140.

[90]Ibid., 143.

[91]Tibesar, *Writings of Junípero Serra*, 1:327, 389.

[92]Ibid., 2:177.

[93]Herbert Bolton, *Font's Complete Diary* (Berkeley: University of California Press, 1933), 301.

[94]Tibesar, *Writings of Junípero Serra*, 2:147.

[95]Ibid., 1:383.

[96]Ibid., 2:139.

[97]Geiger, *Palóu's Life of Fray Junípero Serra*, 167; and Tibesar, *Writings of Junípero Serra*, 3:191.

[98]Tibesar, *Writings of Junípero Serra*, 2:405, 407.

[99]Ibid., 3:253, 423, 425.

[100]Geiger, *Palóu's Life of Fray Junípero Serra*, 285-86.

[101]Ibid., 286.

[102]Tibesar, *Writings of Junípero Serra*, 2:413.

[103]Geiger, *Palóu's Life of Fray Junípero Serra*, 277.

[104]Tibesar, *Writings of Junípero Serra*, 2:143.

[105]Ibid., 4:414.

[106]Geiger, *Palóu's Life of Fray Junípero Serra*, 178.

[107]Tibesar, *Writings of Junípero Serra*, 2:141-42, 3:113, 115.

[108]Ibid., 3:294-95.

[109]Ibid., 3:357.

[110]Ibid., 3:181.

[111]Ibid., 3:99.

[112]Ibid., 4:147.

[113]Mission San Carlos Borromeo *Libro de Difuntos*, Diocese of Monterey Chancery Archives, vol. 1, verso 24.

[114]Tibesar, *Writings of Junípero Serra*, 4:271.

[115]Ibid., 4:275.

[116]Ibid.

[117]Ibid., 4:223.

[118]Ibid., 2:321.

[119]Ibid., 4:289, 291.

[120]Geiger, *Palóu's Life of Fray Junípero Serra*, 243.

[121]Ibid., 244.

[122]Ibid.

[123]Ibid.

[124]Ibid., 245.

[125]Ibid.; and Bolton, *Historical Memoirs of New California*, 4:356-57.

[126]Geiger, *Palóu's Life of Fray Junípero Serra*, 245.

[127]Ibid., 247.

[128]Ibid.
[129]Ibid.
[130]Ibid.
[131]Ibid., 248.
[132]Ibid.

CALIFORNIA PHOTOGRAPHS

[133]"Serra Palm Falls to Power Saw," *The San Diego Union*, 7 June 1957, p. 14.
[134]"1771 Inventario de la Misión de San Diego de Alcalá," Kurt Baer Notes, Santa Barbara Mission Archive-Library.
[135]Tibesar, *Writings of Junípero Serra*, 1:189.
[136]Ibid., 1:191.
[137]Robert E. Cowan Collection, Bancroft Library, University of California, Berkeley, manuscript CC237, p. 3.
[138]Bolton, *Historical Memoirs of New California*, 2:289.
[139]"Historic Oak Tree is Dead," *Monterey New Era*, 6 July 1904, p. 3.
[140]"Historic Oak to be Preserved," *Monterey New Era*, 4 October 1905, p. 1.
[141]Tibesar, *Writings of Junípero Serra*, 3:111.
[142]Bolton, *Historical Memoirs of New California*, 4:50.
[143]"1770 Memoria, Mission San Carlos de Monte Rey," Kurt Baer Notes, Santa Barbara Mission Archive-Library.
[144]Tibesar, *Writings of Junípero Serra*, 2:243.
[145]Geiger, *Palóu's Life of Fray Junípero Serra*, 101.
[146]Tibesar, *Writings of Junípero Serra*, 1:197, 199.
[147]Ibid., 1:222.
[148]Geiger, *Palóu's Life of Fray Junípero Serra*, 110.
[149]Ibid., 110-11.
[150]Bolton, *Historical Memoirs of New California*, 3:224-25.
[151]Tibesar, *Writings of Junípero Serra*, 1:221.
[152]Ibid., 2:431.
[153]Geiger, *Palóu's Life of Fray Junípero Serra*, 116.
[154]"Site of First Mission Cross is Located," *Monterey Peninsula Herald*, 19 December 1939, p. 7.
[155]"Serra's Death Remembered Here Sunday," *Monterey Peninsula Herald*, 26 August 1937, p. 9.
[156]Geiger, *Palóu's Life of Fray Junípero Serra*, 246.
[157]"Carmel Mission Bible to be Used by Reagan," *Monterey Peninsula Herald*, 28 December 1966, p. 1.
[158]Tibesar, *Writings of Junípero Serra*, 2:241-43.
[159]Ibid., 2:241.
[160]Charles Rudkin, ed., *The First French Expedition to California: Lapérouse in 1786* (Los Angeles: Glen Dawson, 1959), 62-63.
[161]Tibesar, *Writings of Junípero Serra*, 3:13.
[162]Ibid., 3:227.
[163]Ibid., 3:357.
[164]Ibid., 2:243.
[165]"Francis Weber, comp. and ed., *The Pride of the Missions: A Documentary History of San Gabriel Mission* (Hong Kong: Libra Press Limited, 1977), 16.
[166]Geiger, *Palóu's Life of Fray Junípero Serra*, 119.
[167]Ibid., 127.
[168]Ibid.
[169]Tibesar, *Writings of Junípero Serra*, 4:261.
[170]Ibid., 1:221.
[171]Bolton, *Historical Memoirs of New California*, 2:300.

[172]Geiger, *Palóu's Life of Fray Junípero Serra*, 134.

[173]Tibesar, *Writings of Junípero Serra*, 2:67.

[174]Ibid., 2:181.

[175]Ibid., 3:247.

[176]Geiger, *Palóu's Life of Fray Junípero Serra*, 80.

[177]Ibid., 201.

[178]"Lo que ha dado el Rey in 1776, Mission San Francisco de Asís," Kurt Baer Notes, Santa Barbara Mission Archive-Library.

[179]"1770 Inventario de la Misión de San Carlos de Monte Rey," *Libro de Cuentas*, Diocese of Monterey Chancery Archives, p. 1.

[180]A.S.C. Forbes, *California Missions and Landmarks* (Los Angeles: A.S.C. Forbes, 1925), 361.

[181]Geiger, *Palóu's Life of Fray Junípero Serra*, 178.

[182]"1782 Informe, Mission San Juan Capistrano," Santa Barbara Mission Archive-Library.

[183]Mission San Carlos Borromeo *Libro de Confirmaciones*, Diocese of Monterey Chancery Archives, entries for 1783.

[184]Tibesar, *Writings of Junípero Serra*, 2:319.

[185]Arthur Spearman, *The Five Mission Churches of Mission Santa Clara: 1777-1825* (Palo Alto: The National Press, 1963), 15.

[186]Ibid., 36.

[187]Ibid., 27.

[188]Ibid., 88; and Arthur Spearman, "Cornerstone Coins of Santa Clara," Santa Clara University Archives, p. 2.

[189]Tibesar, *Writings of Junípero Serra*, 1:222-23.

[190]Geiger, *Palóu's Life of Fray Junípero Serra*, 221-22.

[191]Tibesar, *Writings of Junípero Serra*, 4:114; and Geiger, *The Life and Times of Fray Junípero Serra, O.F.M.*, 2:287.

[192]Bolton, *Historical Memoirs of New California*, 4:214.

POST-MORTEM NARRATIVE

[193]Geiger, *Palóu's Life of Fray Junípero Serra*, 252.

[194]Ibid., 253.

[195]Ibid., 254.

[196]Mission San Carlos Borromeo *Libro de Difuntos*, Diocese of Monterey Chancery Archives, vol. 1, folios 35 and 36.

[197]Geiger, *The Life and Times of Fray Junípero Serra, O.F.M.*, 2:392.

[198]"At San Carlos: Padre Serra's Life Work Commemorated," *San Francisco Chronicle*, 29 August 1884, p. 1.

[199]R.E. White, *Padre Junípero Serra and the Mission Church of San Carlos del Carmelo* (San Francisco: R.E. White, 1884), 27.

[200]*Acceptance and Unveiling of the Statues of Junípero Serra and Thomas Starr King* (Washington, D.C.: United States Government Printing Office, 1932), 56.

[201]Timothy Cardinal Manning, Homily, 28 August 1984, videotape transcript, Mission Carmel Archives.

[202]U.S. Congress, House, "Commemoration of the Father Junípero Serra Bicentennial," 98th Cong., 2nd sess., 21 June 1984, *Congressional Record*, vol. 130, no. 86, page 296.

[203]"Decretum. Montereyen. in California. Canonizationis Ven. Servi Dei Iuniperi Serra, sacerdotis professi, Ordinis Fratrum Minorum, 11 December 1987," Mission Carmel Archives.

[204]Sister Boniface Dyrda to Reverend Noel Moholy, O.F.M., Vice-Postulator, letter, 30 June 1960, p. 1; and Sister Boniface Dyrda to Martin Morgado, letters, 25 February 1988, p. 2, and 22 November 1989, p. 2, Mission Carmel Archives.

[205]"A Visit to Carmel Mission," *Origins: National Catholic Documentary Service* 17 (15 October 1987),311-12.

[206]"Instruction to the Sacred Congregation for the Causes of Saints, dated 20 July 1987," Mission Carmel Archives, p. 1.

[207]"The Way of Holiness is Always the Way of Consecration in the Truth," *L'Osservatore Romano Weekly English Edition*, 24 October 1988, p. 15.

[208]"Mass Honoring Serra Impressive, Beautiful," *The Observer*, 14 September 1989, p. 9.

[209]Imprimatur: Most Reverend Thaddeus Shubsda, Bishop of Monterey in California.

POST-MORTEM PHOTOGRAPHS

[210]Ibid., 4:365-66.

[211]Geiger, *Palóu's Life of Fray Junípero Serra*, 257.

[212]Ibid., ix.

[213]"Report on the Remains Exhumed from the Three Graves in the Church of San Carlos Borromeo de Carmelo, California," in "Transcript of the 13 November 1987 Exhumation of Junípero Serra," Mission Carmel Archives, Appendix B, pp. 31-32.

[214]Maynard Geiger, *Representations of Father Junípero Serra in Painting and Woodcut: Their History and Evaluation* (Santa Barbara: The Franciscan Fathers, 1958), 35.

[215]Francis Farquhar, ed., *Up and Down California in 1860-1864: The Journal of William H. Brewer* (New Haven: Yale University Press, 1930), 106-07.

[216]*Acceptance and Unveiling of the Statues of Junípero Serra and Thomas Starr King*, 21.

[217]Ibid.

[218]Maynard Geiger, "Where is Serra Buried?," *Provincial Annals* 25 (October 1963), 253-54.

[219]Ibid., 26 (January 1964), 77.

[220]Kieran McCarty, "Anniversary of Birth of Fray Junípero Serra," *The Americas* 20 (October 1963), 206-07.

[221]President Ronald Reagan to Most Reverend Thaddeus Shubsda, telegram, 19 August 1985, Mission Carmel Archives.

[222]"Instruction to the Sacred Congregation for the Causes of Saints, dated 20 July 1987," Mission Carmel Archives, p. 2.

[223]*Beatificazione Dei Servi Di Dio Miguel A. Pro, S.J., Martire; Giuseppe B. Dusmet, O.S.B., Vescove; Francesco Faà Di Bruno, Presbitero; Junípero M.J. Serra Ferrer, O.F.M.; Frédéric Janssoone Bollengier, O.F.M.; Josefa Naval Girbés* (Vatican City: Vatican Polyglot Press, 1988), 63-64.

CREDITS: All photographs Patrick Tregenza, Carmel Valley, except: Bancroft Library, Berkeley: Plate 66; Bellerephon Books, Santa Barbara: 105; California Historical Society/Ticor Title Insurance, Los Angeles: 56, 102; California State Library, Sacramento: 63, 128; Kent Connick, San Jose: 51, 106; Convento de San Francisco Archives, Palma: 5; Hubert Lowman, Arroyo Grande: 91; Arturo Mari/*L'Osservatore Romano*, Vatican City: 142, 143; Mission Carmel Archives, Carmel: 78, 100, 118, 123, 124, 126, 129, 130, 131, 132, 137; Monterey Public Library: 64; Martin Morgado, Monterey: 141, 144; Museo Naval, Madrid: 122; Donald Nichols, Carmel: 138; Palo Alto Public Library: 101; Joseph Rimkus, Monterey: back cover; San Diego Historical Society: 54, 57; Santa Barbara Mission Archive-Library: 36, 38; Santa Clara University Archives: 108.

Index

(*def.*) = definition or translation

Junípero Serra Index

135